THE CHURCH OF ST. BUNCO

LECTOR HOUSE PUBLIC DOMAIN WORKS

THE CHURCH OF ST. BUNCO

GORDON CLARK

ISBN: 978-93-5420-920-8

Published: -

LECTOR HOUSE LLP
E-MAIL: lectorpublishing@gmail.com

THE CHURCH OF ST. BUNCO

A DRASTIC TREATMENT OF
A COPYRIGHTED RELIGION—
UN-CHRISTIAN NON-SCIENCE

BY

GORDON CLARK

PREFACE.

The purpose of this book is not to deny the power of mind over matter, or of the human mind over the human body, but to show that the foolish and pestilent thing termed "Christian Science" is a leech fastened upon these great truths, mostly, if not wholly, to batten on them.

There is no use of saying this to "Christian Scientists" themselves—an obedient chain-gang in hypnotic servitude. But people who are not already "in Science" (to use the shibboleth of those who are), ought to be prompted not to get there. The best way in general, I think, is to show that even the historical and biographical claims at the base of the movement are false. If the personal veracity of the head of a church cannot be trusted, "divine revelations," "miracles" and "mental medicine," proceeding from such a source, will naturally be accepted only by the very soft, or else by the very hard for solid considerations.

Is there no sincerity, then, in "Christian Science"? Of course there is. Even the "discoverer and founder" of it undoubtedly believes certain of its asseverations. Mrs. Mary Baker Eddy must be credited, for instance, with the conviction that she has some knowledge of "metaphysics"—a conviction that is nothing worse than a pitiable mistake, which is exploded here at some length. When, as a result of this mistake, she teaches that matter is nothing—not even a condition of anything— only sincerity can account for such lunacy. Yet herein "Christian Science" has its whole rational, or rather irrational, breath of life.

Some "Christian Scientists" sincerely believe in an equivalent for "black magic." As, in their view, "concentration of mind" can cure disease, they think it can also throw disease upon enemies, or upon backsliders from "science." It has been suggested even to the present writer that illness might be cast upon him if he antagonized "the true faith." According to certain dissidents from "Christian Science," "black magic," though with much talk of "chastening love"—(every crime of religious hypocrisy is always committed in the name of "love")—has been persistently tried on heretical wanderers. In the natural course of time some of them are dead; but those whom I have met are not only living, they are comfortably fat.

As "Christian Science" has to me no genuine basis, either in facts, science, theology, metaphysics or therapeutics, but is a mendacious, contradictory, pretentious humbug, I do not hesitate to use such weapons, whether narration, logic, or satire, as are adapted to puncture it. We hear that "Christian Science" has done good. So it has, in some instances, but only through means which it pretends to repudiate, and through the trustful ignorance of those who have been duped by it. We hear, also, that "Christian Scientists" are specially "educated and intelligent." I deny it. No one of them seems ever to have heard of the history of philosophy—a cemetery in which have long lain buried the most of "Mother" Eddy's "divine revelations," "original discoveries" and "absolute demonstrations." Her followers can doubtless *read*, or they would not be available as purchasers of her *Science and Health*; but, if they could *think*, they never would have read the book through. From beginning to end, it is simply a batch of self-contradictions and self-nullities. These are capped with the most impudent claim ever uttered on earth—the claim that the human mind in its natural state cannot comprehend the divine mind incarnate in the author. If caustic is applied to such nonsense, there is no need of apology. The only doubt is that the malefaction is worth the burning.

G. C.

CONTENTS

THE CHURCH OF ST. BUNCO

CHAPTER I.

A BIRD'S-EYE VIEW OF THE THING.

The date of this writing is the year 1901.

About a quarter of a century ago, Boston, the city of modified Puritans and keen business thrift, evolved a new religion. Modern Boston, however, being nothing if not "scientific," the new religion tipped its wings with the new time, and soared aloft in the name of "Christian Science."

In a world not quite converted to this "science," facts sometimes fall behind assertions. But the sect of Christian Science now claims to number in its fold a million sheep. The "mother church," of course, is in Boston; but daughter churches of every age and size are budding and blooming throughout the earth. At headquarters Christian Science has its official weekly organ, its official monthly magazine, and its official publishing house. The cult has issued innumerable books, but specially the multifarious editions of *Science and Health*, the chief work of the adored "mother" and "founder" of Christian Science, Mrs. Mary Baker G. Eddy. As the latest edition of this sacred book is always the best, and as the holy author carefully recommends it as such to all the faithful—whatever other editions they possess—its very high price, under copyright,[1] as compared with undivine books, has rendered it a magnificent source of income. Then, as the average fee for blessing a disciple of Christian Science with a dozen lessons in "metaphysics" and "healing" has been three hundred dollars,[2] a grateful providence through long years, has not only provided food and raiment for "Mother Eddy," but a rich abundance, too, of such worldly goods as should adorn and stimulate perfect piety, not excepting the whitest of diamonds, as symbols of purity, for herself and the elect of her household. Why not? Her devotees are strict adherents of Scripture—always as she interprets it for them—and she believes, for all the text will yield, that "the laborer is worthy of his hire."

Now, apart from the name and the church of Christian Science, there are many people in Boston and its universal radiations—very intelligent and honest people, too—who utterly discard Mrs. Eddy and her teachings, yet hold the general doctrine on which she speculates—the now well-known doctrine that mind governs matter, and that the soul can cure the body of disease. The teaching of these people

[1] From $3.18 to $6.

[2] Mrs. Eddy's statement in her book, *Retrospection and Introspection*, p. 61.

may simply be termed "mental healing," though they say also "mental science," sometimes "metaphysics" and comprehensively "the new thought."

Of late much has been said and written against Christian Science; but adverse criticism has proceeded mostly from physicians in the interest of their schools and theologians in the interest of their creeds. These good souls have taken Christian Science seriously, like the innocent followers of Mrs. Eddy herself. But as soon as a general investigator touches the fad, especially the history of it, he sees that, whatever its effects may have been—good, bad or indifferent—it began in false pretenses,[3] has been pushed for money, and is one of the most shallow humbugs that ever tricked an epoch in the cloak of religion, or reduced "metaphysics" to lunacy. Hence our title. The Church of St. Bunco is the name for the thing. "Christian Science," properly named, is simply *Un*-Christian *Non*-Science.

---

[3] For proof in detail see Chapters III. and IV.

CHAPTER II.

THE ORIGIN OF THE NEW THOUGHT.[4]

"Christian Science," "Mental Healing," "Metaphysical Treatment of Disease," —where did these things come from, and how did they get here? The facts are peculiar; they are partly unpleasant; they are sometimes amusing; but they are not far to seek.

In 1836, Charles Poyan, a Frenchman, introduced into the United States the practise of Mesmerism. In 1840 it was taken up, with great earnestness, by a Maine Yankee, named Phineas Parkhurst Quimby. He was a watch and clock maker, an inventor, and a natural reformer. In making his mesmeric experiments, he soon found an extraordinary subject of them in the person of a young man, Lucius Burkmar, with whom he traveled several years, giving, it is said, some of the most astonishing exhibitions of mesmerism and clairvoyance that had ever been known. As the substance of mesmerism, though under the newer name of hypnotism, has now been fully substantiated by the French Academy of Medicine, the highest authority in the world on such subjects, there seems to be no longer any reasonable question of its general claims.

On taking up mesmerism in New England, Mr. Quimby had been very ill and given up by his physicians to die. By inquiring into his own condition through his clairvoyant subject, Lucius, and by the young man's laying-on of hands, Mr. Quimby, as he tells the story, recovered immediately from a long-standing and dangerous malady. Partly as a result of this cure, but much more because his whole life shows him to have been a natural exemplar of "the good physician," he took to "healing the sick." He held no diploma from any college of medicine; but his work and his thousands of patients inevitably conferred upon him the title of "Doctor."

At first he merely co-operated with the regular medical faculty, who sometimes called upon him to have his subject, Lucius, examine their patients. Being put into the mesmeric state, young Burkmar would describe the disease, with the pains accompanying it, and would then go on and prescribe remedies, though he knew nothing about them.

As a participant and student of this process, Dr. Quimby came, in a short time, to the conclusion that the diagnosis of the clairvoyant was not necessarily the true

---

[4] Our historical sources of information are referred to as we go along, but a good deal of it has come from access to original documents, and from living persons of the highest character who were long and intimately acquainted with the subject of our chapter. The names of some of these friends are given by permission.

one, but was taken from the belief of the patient, or his physician, or some other person, and was, therefore, an impression of incidental mind, rather than a statement of fact. Such results would not do for a man like Quimby; so he dismissed mesmerism — such practise of it at least as depended on anybody but himself and those on whom he directly operated. Meanwhile, according to the best of testimony, there was developed in himself a faculty much more peculiar and effective than ordinary "mind-reading" and "second-sight." Gradually, too, he formed an entirely new and original theory of disease. In 1857, in a Maine paper, the *Bangor Jeffersonian*, his faculty and his theory were described thus:

"It is universally acknowledged that the mind is often the cause of disease, but it has never been supposed to have an equal power in overcoming it. Quimby's theory is that the mind gives immediate form to the animal spirit, and that the animal spirit gives form to the body.... Therefore, his first course in the treatment of a patient is to sit down beside him, and put himself *en rapport* with him, which he does without producing the mesmeric sleep.... With the spirit form Dr. Quimby converses and endeavors to win it away from its grief; and, when he has succeeded in doing so, it disappears, and reunites with the body. Thus is commenced the first step towards recovery.... This union frequently lasts but a short time, when the spirit again appears, exhibiting some new phase of its troubles. With this he again contends until he overcomes it, when it disappears as before. Thus two shades of trouble have disappeared from the mind, and consequently from the animal spirit; and the body has already commenced its efforts to come into a state in accordance with them."

In an article written by Dr. Quimby himself (in 1861), he explained his procedure in this way:

"A patient comes to see Dr. Quimby. He renders himself absent to everything but the impression of the person's feelings. These are quickly daguerreotyped on him. They contain no intelligence, but shadow forth a reflection of themselves which he looks at. This contains the disease as it appears to the patient. Being confident that it is the shadow of a false idea, he (Dr. Quimby) is not afraid of it.... Then his feelings in regard to the disease, which are health and strength, are daguerreotyped on the receptive plate of the patient, which also throws forth a shadow. The patient, seeing this shadow of the disease in a new light, gains confidence. This change of feeling is daguerreotyped on the doctor again. This also throws forth a shadow, and he sees the change, and continues to treat it in the same way. So the patient's feelings sympathize with his, the shadow changes and grows dim, and finally disappears. The light takes its place, and there is nothing left of the disease."

Dr. Quimby was not an educated man in the technical meaning of the term; but, through his experiments in mesmerism and his personal experiences, he was led directly to what in the history of philosophy is called "absolute idealism." Until his own conclusions were fully reached, he knew nothing, from literature, even of Berkeley; but when Berkeley's writings were unfolded to him, he at once said, in his plain, straightforward way, that they were true, and that he "agreed" with them. To him, the universe was mind, and all things were "ideas." Disease was an "idea," though he sometimes called it "matter," as being *negative mind*, or that which "*could receive impressions*" and "*be changed by them*." Hence he said:

"The idea (disease) is matter; and it decomposes, and throws off an odor that contains all the ideas of the person affected. This is true of every idea or thought. Now my odor comes in contact with this odor, and I, being well, have found out by twenty years' experience that these odors affect me, and also that they contain the very identity of the patient whom this odor surrounds. This called my attention to it; and I found that it was as easy to tell the feelings or thoughts of a sick person as to detect the odor of spirits from that of tobacco. I at first thought I inhaled it, but at last found that my senses could be affected by it when my body was at a distance of many miles from the patient. This led to a new discovery; and I found that my senses were not in my body, but that my body was in my senses. My knowledge located my senses just according to my wisdom. If a man's knowledge is in matter, all there is of him is contained in matter. But, if his knowledge is in wisdom, then his senses and all there is of him are out of matter."

In 1860 Dr. Quimby used, in Portland and vicinity, a circular addressed "to the sick," some copies of which have been preserved, and from an original copy of which the following extracts are taken:

"Dr. P. P. Quimby would respectfully announce that he will attend to those wishing to consult him in regard to their health, and, as his practice is unlike all other medical practice, it is necessary to say that he gives no medicine *and makes no outward applications*, but simply sits down by the patients, tells them their feelings, &c., then his explanation is the cure; and, if he succeeds in correcting their error, he changes the fluids of the system and establishes the truth, or health. *The Truth is the Cure.* This mode of treatment applies to all cases. If no explanation is given, no charge is made, for no effect is produced.... If patients feel pain they know it, and, if he describes their pain, he feels it.... After this it becomes his duty to prove to them the cause of their trouble.... This has been his mode of practice for the last seventeen years. For the past eight years he has given no medicines, nor made any outward applications.... There are many who pretend to practice as he does; but when a person, while in a trance, claims any power from the spirits of the departed, and recommends any kind of medicine to be taken internally or applied externally, beware! Believe them not, 'for by their fruits ye shall know them.'"[5]

In 1887 a short account of Dr. Quimby and his work was published in a pamphlet entitled *The True History of Mental Science*, by Julius A. Dresser. Mr. Dresser had been a patient and friend of Dr. Quimby, who had looked to him to cultivate and extend the Quimby system. But the immediate accomplishment of that purpose had been prevented.

In 1895 Mrs. Annetta Gertrude Dresser, the wife of Julius A. Dresser, and, like him, a patient and personal friend of Dr. Quimby, gave to the public a small but comprehensive volume, *The Philosophy of Dr. P. P. Quimby*.[6] This excellent sketch

[5] This circular alone—furnished to the writer by Dr. Quimby's son—is complete proof as to origin of "mind-healing" in the United States.

[6] The reader is advised to consult the pamphlet and the book here specified, in connection with our chapter. (Geo. H. Ellis, Publisher, Boston)—G. C.

of the man and his career contains part of an article upon him written by his son, Mr. George A. Quimby, for the *New England Magazine* of March, 1888, the article being followed, in Mrs. Dresser's book, by various newspaper notices and criticisms of Dr. Quimby, running from 1857 to 1863, then by reminiscences of him, an exposition of his theories, and by selections from his manuscripts.

The newspaper articles were mostly prepared by grateful patients whom Dr. Quimby had restored from sickness to health.[7] Among these patients were two daughters of Judge Ashur Ware[8] of Portland, Maine, one of whom, Mrs. Sarah Ware Mackay, still lives to bless the good Doctor's memory. The Ware sisters became so deeply interested in Dr. Quimby's thoughts and cures that they persuaded him to write out his ideas and explain his practise. As he was exceedingly busy, his articles were rewritten by the two young ladies or by Mr. George A. Quimby, and were then submitted to the Doctor for correction. His terminology was peculiar, and sometimes inadequate to his meaning; but due attention to his writings, with those of his friends, yields a clear conception of him.

One thing will never be questioned by any honest and sensible person acquainted with the facts: Dr. Quimby's biographers—his son and his trusted friends, the Dressers—have told the truth about him. The information they give fully sustains their general estimate. This estimate established, we know that Dr. Quimby himself was absolutely sincere, and could be fully trusted just so far as he understood his own nature and what he was doing. But this is not to say that he was always right. It is not even to say that he was without the strongest of prejudices, which may sometimes have misled him. He was too broad and high a soul to be *opinionated* in any narrow, selfish sense; but he would stand for a conviction till "the crack of doom." "The old gentleman," says one who knew him familiarly for many years, "would *argue* a sitting hen off her nest."

Reference has been made to his ill-health when he began to study mesmerism. Physicians had told him that his "kidneys were partially consumed," and that he had "ulcers on his lungs."

"On one occasion [he says], when I had my subject asleep, he told me that one [of my kidneys] was half consumed, and a piece three inches long had separated from it, and was only connected by a slender thread. This was what I believed to be true; for it agreed with what the doctors told me, and with what I had suffered—for I had not been free from pain for years. My common sense told me that no medicine would ever cure the trouble, and therefore I must suffer till death relieved me. But I asked [my subject] if there was no remedy. He replied, 'Yes—I can put the piece on so it will grow, and you will get well.'... He placed his hands upon me, and said he united the pieces so they would grow. The next day he said they had grown together; and from that day I never experienced the least pain from them."[9]

---

[7] These press articles and notices have been examined by the writer, and are unmistakably genuine, as are the selections.

[8] U. S. Court of Admiralty. Judge Ware was sometimes spoken of as the leading citizen of Maine.

[9] *The True History of Mental Science*, page 15.

Dr. Quimby's personal veracity being accepted by the present writer as unimpeachable, his word must be taken as perfectly good for this remarkable story, as he understood the matter. But the various inferences he drew from his case may be questioned, with no disadvantage to his character.

"I concluded" [said he], "that [the subject] read my mind; and *his ideas were so absurd* that *the disease vanished by the absurdity of the cure.*"

It appears that this mesmeric subject, though he could be forced, under control, to prescribe anything in the mind of the operator, always did prescribe, if left to himself, some very simple remedy.

"When I mesmerized my subject," says Dr. Quimby, "he would prescribe some little simple herb that would do no harm or good of itself. In some cases this would cure the patient. I also found that any medicine would cure certain cases if he ordered it. This led me to investigate the matter, and arrive at the stand that the cure is not in the medicine, but in the confidence of the doctor or medium."

In his early invalid life, Dr. Quimby had been "filled," he tells us, with "calomel" and other "strong doses of allopathic poison." As we read his description of Lucius and the "simple herbs," the thought arises that the mesmeric subject might have had some power or aid after all, that his good operator passed over too cavalierly, and that the "herbs" might have appeared more efficacious, if a reminiscence of vigorous "blue pills," in which Dr. Quimby once had confidence, had not still dwelt on his tongue. It is certain that, since his time, some very sensible persons believe they have been cured of so dire an affliction as cancer by so innocent a concoction as clover tea.

Dr. Quimby, to use the language of his first biographer, Mr. Dresser, "progressed gradually out of mesmerism, into a knowledge of the hidden powers of mind; and he soon found in man a principle, or a power, that was not of man himself, but was higher than man, and of which he could only be a medium. Its character was goodness and intelligence; and its power was great. He also found that disease was nothing but an erroneous belief of mind.... On this discovery he founded a system of treating the sick, and founded a science of life.... His discovery was not made from the Bible, but from natural phenomena and searching investigation.... After the truth was discovered, he found his new views all portrayed and illustrated in Christ's teachings and works."

Some of these claims were reaffirmed by Dr. Quimby himself, in a letter written in 1860.[10]

"You inquire [he says] if I have ever cured any cases of chronic rheumatism. I answer, Yes; but ... you cannot be saved by pinning your faith on another's sleeve. Every one must answer for his own sins or belief. Our beliefs are the cause of our misery, and our happiness or misery is what follows our belief.... You ask if my practice belongs to any known science. My answer is, No; it belongs to a Wisdom that is above man as man.... It was taught eighteen hundred years ago, and has never had a place in the heart of man since, but is in the world, and the world knows it not."

[10] Philosophy of P. P. Quimby, page 53-54.

In *The Philosophy of P. P. Quimby*, we are told that

> "It was Dr. Quimby's chief aim to establish a science of life
> and happiness, which all could learn, and which should relieve
> humanity of sickness and misery."

But after our various quotations, we can readily perceive, as his biographer maintains, that "by the word, 'science,'" he always meant "not what is commonly understood by that word, but something spiritual." By "science," in short, or what he sometimes called "Wisdom," Dr. Quimby meant simply the principle of the universe, the presence, truth and power of God, at the foundation of the human soul.

Dr. Quimby said, and his disciples have said after him, that he "never went into any trance," and was "a strong disbeliever in *Spiritualism*, as understood by that name." Pursuing this statement in detail, we find that his criticism of the subject consisted mostly in his denying the accuracy of information derived from clairvoyants and spirit-mediums. But, in the words of one of his most intimate friends, he considered our two states of physical and spiritual life as "only a difference in dissolving views," and he believed that his own thought and senses existed, a part of the time, out of matter, or in "the scientific world."[11] He even affirmed, in connection with his view of disease as an impression of mind, that, transferring himself into the spiritual state of existence, he had cured his own parents, *after death*, of ailments which had not left them when they departed from their physical condition. To this strange man, Dr. Quimby, the world of matter and the world of spirit were so interblended as to be only two phases of the same thing, *both of which he constantly experienced.*

"What," he asks, "is this body that we see?" It is "a tenement for man to occupy *when he pleases*. But, as a man knows not himself, he reasons as though he were one of the fixtures of his house, or body.... What is the true definition of death. Death is the name of an idea.... So the destruction of an idea is death." Man "is dying and living all the time to error, till he dies the death of all his opinions and beliefs. Therefore to be free from death is to be alive in truth." In no other way than this, would Dr. Quimby even recognize such a fact as death. When he came to die himself, he said "I am perfectly willing for the *change*.... But I know that I shall be *right here with you, just the same as I have always been*. I do not dread the change any more than if I were going on a trip to Philadelphia."

Dr. Quimby, then, in his own way, certainly did believe, accept and avow what is commonly understood as Spiritualism, but he repudiated its frequently doubtful accompaniments.

"I know [said he] just how much reliance can be placed on a medium; for when in the mesmeric state, they are governed by the superstition and beliefs of the person they are in communication with.... The capacity of thought-reading is the common extent of mesmerism. Clairvoyance is very rare.... This state is of very short duration. They then come into that state where they are governed by surrounding minds. All the mediums of this day reason about medicine as much

---

[11] Mrs. Sarah Ware Mackay.

as the regular physician. *They believe in disease and recommend medicine."*

Here we have it, exactly. Dr. Quimby did *not* believe in disease, except as "an error of mind," and did *not* recommend medicine. So, while he accepted spirit-condition, to the fullest extent, he refused to accept information from it at second hand. He held that, because a man had "passed over to the other side," as the Spiritualists say, he was not necessarily any wiser than he had been in "mind reduced to a state called matter."

"The invisible world [said he] opens all the avenues of matter, through which to give the inhabitants communications; but the natural man has possession of the mediums, so that the scientific man is misrepresented in nine-tenths of all he says. Now to be in the scientific world is not necessarily to be wise, but to acknowledge a wisdom above the natural man, which will enter the world where wisdom sees through matter. This is the condition of those persons who are thrown into a clairvoyant state. To them, matter is nothing but an idea, that is seen or not, just as it is called out. All their senses are in this state, but are under the control of the natural man.... The explanation of the scientific world is given by these blind guides ... who cannot understand science."

From this last quotation, we can see precisely how Dr. Quimby at once accepted and rejected Spiritualism; and we can see, as well, how he reached the posture of rational idealism. As far as concerned his powers or gifts, the good man was what would now be called a "mesmerist," a "clairvoyant," and a "healing medium" — only he was of so sensitive a spiritual nature that he could exercise these faculties "in his senses," or in what, *to him*, was "a perfectly normal state." If, to his own direct vision and experience, "matter" was "nothing but an idea," to be "seen or not, just as it is called out," his conclusion could only be that "all that is seen by the natural man is mind reduced to a state called matter," and that "there is no matter independent of mind, or life."

But even if granting this posture as a philosophical premise, is it a logical conclusion to insist, with Dr. Quimby, that disease is merely "a belief," and that "health is wisdom?"

"I deny disease as a truth," said he, but "admit it as a deception. Disease is an evil that follows taking an opinion for a truth. Every disease is an invention of man, and has no identity in wisdom.... Disease is the misery of our belief, happiness is the health of our wisdom.... False reasoning is sickness and death.... The devil is the error of mankind.... We are made up of truth and error. Disease is an error, or belief; the Truth is the cure."

It is necessary to explain, however, that Dr. Quimby found the cause of human misery "not alone in the conscious mind" and the "opinions and beliefs about disease," but in the "mental influences and thoughts by which every person is surrounded," and in the "unconscious or subconscious mind." He declared that he could tell "an idea or cause" of sickness from the sensation produced by it, "just as a person knows an orange by the odor." As he "was able to do this," says Mr. Dresser, "he always told the patient, at the first sitting, what the latter thought was his disease, and never allowed the patient to tell him anything about the case."

In a later chapter of our book, the hypothesis that because, in the last analysis "all things are mind," all disease can be cured by mind *while it exists in the body*, will be carefully considered. Meanwhile it must be admitted, without reserve, that under this doctrine, which Dr. Quimby himself believed with all his might, he practised "healing," for many years, with marvelous success.

He labored, too, under great difficulties. Fifty years ago, the average inhabitant of New England was not quite so bigoted and superstitious, perhaps, as the Jews in the time of Christ, but quite enough so to suggest a comparison. Dr. Quimby was not orthodox in his theology, and was still less orthodox in medicine. As Mr. Dresser records the situation,

"[Those] who were then willing to try a practitioner outside of the medical schools, were persons who had exhausted every means of help within those schools, and, when finally booked for the grave, would send or go to Quimby."

In the way of a "grim joke," the Doctor himself said that his patients "would send for him and the undertaker at the same time, and the one who got there first would get the case." And the worst of it all was that his power, when acknowledged, was frequently "imputed to the devil." Still, he had more work than he could do—so much that it wore him completely out, and finally ended his life at the age of sixty-four. In his busiest days, he said:

"I have sat with more than three hundred individuals every year for ten years, and for the last five years I have averaged five hundred yearly—people with all sorts of diseases, and every possible state of mind, brought on by all kinds of ideas in which people believe. Religion in its various forms embraces many of these causes. Some cases have been occasioned by the idea that [the patients] had committed the unpardonable sin. When asked what it was, no two persons ever answered alike."

There is no doubt that Dr. Quimby's patients were generally cured, unless he told them at once that they were past his or any other mortal aid. "He saw through them at a glance," as all who knew him agree in testifying. To deceive him was impossible. For instance: A lady who scouted his special vision, and was in good health, went to him feigning illness, and for the purpose of a test. "He received her, as he would any one, and, after a few moments, without a word having been spoken, took his chair, and, placing it before her, sat down with his back to her, saying: 'That is the way you feel toward me. I think you don't need my services, and had better go home.'" A patient and friend—an eye-witness of unquestionable veracity—says:

"People were coming to Dr. Quimby from all parts of New England. Many of these came on crutches, or were assisted into the office; and it was most interesting to note their progress day by day, or the remarkable change produced by a single sitting.... I remember one lady who had used crutches for twenty years, who walked without them after a few weeks."

There is now living in Boston a gentleman who happens to be personally known to the present writer. The gentleman is a college graduate of high culture, of large experience, and with the rest, is an author of distinction. When a young man he had a serious affliction of the eyes, which gradually increased until he was threatened with blindness. He was a man of means, and no expense was spared to secure the best medical treatment. It was unavailing. He heard of Dr. Quimby, and, as the usual "last resort," applied to him. "He cured me," says the gentleman, "and I have had no trouble since. But how he did it I don't know. He sat and talked with me, and sometimes touched my head and face with his hands, moistened with cold water, though declaring even this to be of no vital consequence. He cured other people of all sorts of things, as easily as he cured me. Here I am with two good eyes, and you have the facts."[12]

The ultimate value of "The New Thought," or "Mental and Moral Healing," is yet a problem; but that P. P. Quimby was the spring and fountain of the whole stream, with its various branches, is beyond all reputable dispute. It rests on these grounds:

First. He claimed it himself in the presence of all whom he met, spreading the claim broadcast even in newspaper advertisements and business circulars.

Second. Many of the most intelligent and trustworthy of his patients became, as we have seen, correspondents of the press to express their gratitude for his cures, and scores of their articles have been preserved. With no exception, these articles substantiate Dr. Quimby's declaration that he alone, of all persons then living, treated disease through the normal action of the human mind.

Third. Dr. Quimby had a son, Mr. George A. Quimby, who acted for years as his father's secretary. This gentleman is living, and is a well and widely known citizen of Belfast, Maine. His distinct claim for Dr. Quimby is that "up to his time, no man, since Jesus, had attempted and succeeded in curing the sick, without medicine, applications, mesmerism, hypnotism or spiritualism, simply mentally—through the mind and sense—and who further claimed that he did it in a scientific manner which could be taught to others, ... and was in a normal state of mind all the time, as also was his patient."

Fourth. A number of Dr. Quimby's patients and close friends long survived him, and several of them still live. With a single exception, every one of these people has said, in substance, exactly what Mr. George A. Quimby states in detail.

Fifth. The single exception is a lady who once said what all the rest say—and who *is completely on record as saying it*—but who, for reasons easy to understand and explain, has since taken a lady's high and mighty privilege of "changing her mind." We will inspect this change.

---

[12] The gentleman is Hon. Edwin Reed, of Boston, Mass. His name is given by his permission, from a feeling of gratitude to Dr. Quimby, and profound respect for his memory.

CHAPTER III.

DR. QUIMBY'S MOST DISTINGUISHED PATIENT.

Dr. Quimby was at the height of his career during the early days of our Civil War. Among his patients at that time was one who has since become the most celebrated of them, and who now bears the name of Mary Baker Glover Eddy. Then, however, the patient was known as Mary M. Patterson—an incident which occurred through her being a very energetic and pious woman, who has attracted to herself a considerable variety of husbands.[13] It was in 1862, says Dr. Quimby's biographer, Mrs. A. G. Dresser, "that Mrs. Eddy, author of *Science and Health*, was associated with Dr. Quimby; and I well remember the very day when she was helped up the steps of his office on the occasion of her first visit. She was cured by him, and afterward became very much interested in his theory. But she put her own construction on much of his teaching, and developed a system of thought which differed radically from it."

Mrs. Mary Baker G. Patterson (since Mrs. Eddy), was greatly surprised at her cure, and naturally grateful for it. She at once said so in print. It was in an issue of the Portland Evening *Courier*, of November 7th, 1862. Her account was this:

"Three weeks ago I quitted my nurse and sick-room *en route* for Portland. The belief of my recovery had died out of the hearts of those who were most anxious for it. With this mental and physical depression, I first visited P. P. Quimby, and in less than one week from that time I ascended by a stairway of one-hundred and eighty-two steps to the dome of the City Hall, and am improving *ad infinitum*.... I have employed electro-magnetism and animal magnetism, and for a brief period I have felt relief ... but in no instance did I get rid of a return of all my ailments, because I had not been helped out of the error in which opinions involve us. My operator believed in disease independent of mind; hence I could not be wiser than my teacher. But now I can see, dimly at first, and only as trees walking, the great principle which underlies Dr. Quimby's faith and works; and just in proportion to my right perception of truth is my recovery. This truth, which he opposes to the error of giving intelligence to matter and placing pain where it never placed itself, if received understandingly, changes the currents of the system to their normal action, and the mechanism of the body goes on undisturbed. That this is a science capable of demonstration becomes clear to the minds of those patients who reason upon the process of their cure. The truth which he establishes in the patient cures him (although he may be wholly unconscious thereof), and the body, which is full

---

[13] Mrs. Eddy's complete name, with reference to these gentlemen, would be Mary Baker Glover Patterson Eddy.

of light, is no longer in disease."

The communication of Mrs. Mary Baker G. Eddy—then Mrs. Mary M. Patterson—which she published in the Portland *Courier*, was criticised, the next day, November 8th, 1862, by the Portland *Advertiser*. In reply to that paper she said:

"P. P. Quimby stands upon the plain of wisdom with his truth. Christ healed the sick, but not by jugglery or with drugs. As the former speaks as never man before spake, and heals as never man healed since Christ, is he not identified with truth, and is not this the Christ which is in him?... P. P. Quimby rolls away the stone from the sepulcher of error, and health is the resurrection.... But light shineth in darkness, and the darkness comprehendeth it not."[14]

Dr. Quimby having died on the 16th of January, 1866, Mrs. M. B. G. Patterson—not to be Mrs. M. B. G. Patterson Eddy until 1867—"sent to me," says Mr. Julius Dresser in his *True History of Mental Science*, "a copy of a poem she had written to his memory." With the poem was sent the following letter:

Lynn, February 15, 1866.

Mr. Dresser:

"*Sir*,—I enclose some lines of mine in memory of our much loved friend, which perhaps *you* will not think overwrought in meaning: *others* must, of course.

"I am constantly wishing that *you* would step forward into the place he has vacated. I believe you would do a vast amount of good, and are more capable of occupying his place than any other I know of.

"Two weeks ago I fell on the sidewalk and struck my back on the ice and was taken up for dead, came to consciousness amid a storm of vapors from cologne, chloroform, ether, camphor, etc., but to find myself the helpless cripple I was before I saw Dr. Quimby.

"The physician attending said I had taken the last step I ever should, but in two days I got out of my bed *alone*, and *will* walk; but yet I confess I am frightened, and out of that nervous heat my friends are forming, spite of me, the terrible spinal affection from which I have suffered so long and hopelessly.... Now can't *you* help me? I believe you can. I write this with this feeling: I think that I could help another in my condition if they had not placed their intelligence in matter. This I have not done, and yet I am slowly failing. Won't you write me if you will undertake for me if I can get to you?...

"Respectfully,
"Mary M. Patterson."

The poem by the lady destined to become Mrs. Eddy, author of *Science and*

---

[14] The writer has had these records authenticated at Portland.—G. C.

Health, was published by her, with her name attached, under the caption of

> "LINES on the death of Dr. P. P. Quimby, *who healed with the Truth*
> *that Christ taught, in contradistinction to all Isms.*"

> "Did sackcloth clothe the sun, and day grow night,
> All matter mourn the hour with dewy eyes,
> When Truth, receding from our mortal sight,
> Had paid to error her last sacrifice?

> "Can we forget the power that gave us life?
> Shall we forget the wisdom of its way?
> Then ask me not amid this mortal strife—
> This keenest pang of animated clay—

> "To mourn him less: to mourn him more were just,
> If to his memory 'twere a tribute given
> For every solemn, sacred, earnest trust
> Delivered to us ere he rose to heaven—

> "Heaven but the happiness of that calm soul,
> Growing in stature to the throne of God.
> Rest should reward him who hath made us whole,
> Seeking, tho' tremblers, where his footsteps trod."

MARY M. PATTERSON.

The complete identity of Mrs. Mary M. Patterson with Mrs. Mary Baker G. Eddy has been fully established by the highest Christian-Science authority in the world—Mrs. Eddy herself. In a letter dated March 7th, 1883, addressed to the Boston *Post*, she said:

"In 1862 my name was Patterson, my husband, Dr. Patterson, a distinguished dentist. After our marriage I was confined to my bed with a severe illness, and seldom left bed or room for seven years, when I was taken to Dr. Quimby and partially restored. I returned home, hoping once more to make that home happy, but only returned to a new agony to find that my husband had eloped with a married woman from one of the wealthy families of that city, leaving no trace save his last letter to us, wherein he wrote: 'I hope some time to be worthy of so good a wife.' I have a bill of divorce from him...."

In her letter to the Boston *Post* Mrs. Eddy made some other interesting assertions. She said:[15]

> "We never were a student of Dr. Quimby. Dr. Quimby never
> had students to our knowledge. He was somewhat of a remark-
> able healer, and at the time we knew him he was known as a mes-
> merist. We were one of his patients."

What an astonishing look these statements by Mrs. Eddy in 1883 have, when compared with the statements of Mrs. Mary M. Patterson from 1862 to 1866. Let

---

[15] The original print has been in my hands. A copy of the letter is published in full in *The True History of Mental Science* (Appendix A).—G. C.

us see. —

Statement of 1883.

"At the time we knew him [Dr. Quimby], he was known as a mesmerist."

Statement of 1866.

"Dr. Quimby healed with the truth that Christ taught, in contradistinction to all Isms."

"Rest should reward him who hath made us whole, *seeking, tho' tremblers, where his footsteps trod.*"

On March 7th, 1883, Mrs. Mary Baker G. Eddy made, in the Boston Post.

This Statement.

"We had laid the foundation of mental healing long before we ever saw Dr. Quimby.... We made our first experiments in mental healing about 1853, when we were convinced that mind had a science which, if understood, would heal all diseases."

In October, 1862, the same lady, through the Portland *Courier*, made

This Statement.

"I can see, *dimly at first and as trees walking,* the great principle which underlies Dr. Quimby's faith and works; and just in proportion to my right perception of truth is my recovery. This truth, which he opposes to *the error of giving intelligence to matter,* changes the currents of the system. The truth which he establishes in the patient cures him. This is a science capable of demonstration to those who reason upon the process."

Then, in the Portland *Advertiser*, came Mrs. Eddy's extraordinary comparison of Dr. Quimby's words and deeds with those of Christ, and

This Statement.

"P. P. Quimby rolls away the stone from the sepulcher of error, and health is the resurrection."

On the publication of Julius A. Dresser's *True History of Mental Science*—to which reference has been made in our previous chapter—Mrs. Eddy was greatly exercised over it. In her *Christian Science Journal* for June, 1887, she devoted the leading article, under her own name, to the Dresser pamphlet.

This little thing was a calm statement of facts, proved as they were given. From the facts, Dr. Quimby's theory was drawn, and Mr. Dresser frankly recounted what the general reader would consider Dr. Quimby's foibles and prejudices, as well as his doctrines and gifts. The pamphlet contained Mrs. Mary M. Patterson's opinion of Dr. Quimby in 1862, and her poem of 1866. It agreed with what was then the substance of her own assertions, by summarizing Dr. Quimby "as the first person of this age who penetrated the depths of truth so far as to discover and bring forth a true science of life, and openly apply it to the healing of the sick."

But, in criticising Mr. Dresser's quiet monograph, the amiable "Mother of Christian Science," proclaimed that Mr. Dresser had "let loose the dogs of war."; had unleashed a "pet poodle," alternately "to bark and whine" at her "heels"; and she identified the "pet poodle" with a certain "sucking litterateur," who had renounced allegiance to her.[16] But when her preliminary high-tide had ebbed a little, her pen dropped this:

"Did I write those articles in Mr. Dresser's pamphlet, purporting to be mine? I might have written them, twenty or thirty years ago, for I was under the mesmeric treatment of Dr. Quimby from 1862 until his death, in 1865. He was illiterate, and knew nothing then of the science of Mind-healing; and I was as ignorant of mesmerism as Eve before she was tempted by the serpent."

Those Patterson-Eddy "articles," then—no possible mendacity being adequate to their extinction—have been grudgingly and angrily admitted by their author to be genuine. But she would ignore them on the ground of "mesmerism." Her "head," she says, "was so turned by Animal Magnetism and will power" under Dr. Quimby's treatment, that she "might have written something as hopelessly incorrect" as the articles referred to.

But *was* Mrs. Mary M. Patterson under "mesmeric treatment," or *did* Mrs. Mary Patterson Eddy ever really *believe* she was under such treatment, when with Dr. Quimby? And was she then a truly "ignorant Eve," without a fig-leaf of knowledge pertaining to mesmerism? In 1862 she thought *not*, and we have seen that, in writing her first newspaper letter on Dr. Quimby, she turned her thought into these words:

"*I have employed electro-magnetism and animal magnetism*, and for a brief period I have felt relief ... but in no instance did I get rid of a return of all my ailments, *because I had not been helped out of the error in which opinions involve us. My operator believed in disease independent of mind; hence I could not be wiser than my teacher.*"

Mrs. Patterson continued her letter by saying what has already been quoted in full—that Dr. Quimby cured her by "a great principle" of "science," through which he established "the truth" in "the patient"—a truth which he opposed to the error of giving intelligence to matter, and placing pain where it never placed itself.

In Mrs. Eddy's magazine article of June, 1887, she went so far as to say of Dr. Quimby,

"His healing was never *considered* or *called* anything but Mesmerism."

Well, Mrs. Mary M. Patterson, from 1862 to 1866, both "considered" and "called" the Doctor's healing something wholly different from mesmerism; and, saying it was done "by the truth which Christ taught," she considered and called

---

[16] The gentleman here traduced is Dr. L. M. Marston of Boston. He is a practising physician, and a thoughtful, honest man. He is the author of a well-written book entitled, *Essentials of Mental Healing*, which is much superior to *Science and Health*, though containing some of the overdone conceptions of mind-cure in general. But Dr. Marston properly employs material as well as mental medicine.—G. C.

it something "in contradistinction to *all* Isms."

Meanwhile, for more than three years of Mrs. Eddy's close acquaintance with Dr. Quimby, all his advertisements, even, told her, what she then fluently repeated, that he cured disease by implanting *truth* in the human mind, in place of *error*—"the truth being the cure." In other words, everything around her proclaimed that Dr. Quimby's cures were performed wholly by Mind-healing.

Mrs. Eddy's reversal of herself has been so agile and exhaustive since her comparisons of Dr. Quimby with our Lord Jesus Christ, that she has latterly preferred to speak of the good old doctor, who taught and healed her, as "unlearned"—a "mesmerist" who cured a patient by "rubbing" her—an "illiterate" man who said that he was only "John" while she was "Jesus," and whose "scribblings" she, to a considerable extent, wrote herself. From all this it must be adduced that Mrs. Eddy, in her Patterson days, went to Dr. Quimby to be cured of disease, but taught him to do it.

It is true, as we have noted, that Dr. Quimby was not an educated man, in the sense of the schools. It would have been impossible for him to write like Mrs. Eddy. When, for instance, she excogitated that first letter of Mrs. Patterson's to the Portland *Courier*, she opened it in this way:

"When our Shakespeare decided that there were more things in this world 'than were dreamed of in your philosophy,' I cannot say of a verity that he had a foreknowledge of P. P. Quimby. And when the school Platonic anatomized the soul and divided it into halves, to be united by elementary attractions, and heathen philosophers averred that old Chaos in sullen silence brooded o'er the earth until her inimitable form was hatched from the egg of night, I would not at present decide whether the fallacy was found in their premises or conclusions, never having dated my existence before the flood."

No: P. P. Quimby, even if aided by all the freshmen and sophomores that ever lived, could never have risen into the state of gorgeous, ponderous culture evinced in the foregoing power-house and epitome of all learning. Besides, when that incomparable paragraph was erected, Mrs. Eddy was young—not yet fifty years of age. At sixty, her literary *style* had lost something of its dazzle; but, in *matter*, all her work, especially her world-renowned book, *Science and Health*, compares beautifully with her grand production of 1862.

P. P. Quimby was a plain man of great natural genius. When he wrote—generally in great haste—he paid little attention to capital letters, punctuation, or *form* of any kind; but his manuscripts were carefully revised, under his own direction, by his two faithful friends, the Ware sisters, or by his son, Mr. George A. Quimby. Mrs. Mary M. Patterson borrowed and read some occasional jotting—that was all. In the possession of Mr. George A. Quimby are eight hundred pages of his father's writings, prepared before Dr. Quimby had the honor of knowing that Mrs. Patterson (to be Eddy) was on the face of the earth. These writings contain the substance of all his thoughts.

The knowledge that such writings exist has much disturbed Mrs. Mary Baker Glover Patterson Eddy. On the 21st of May, 1887, she published, through a Boston newspaper, an offer to print the Quimby manuscripts, at her own expense, *provided* she should "first *be allowed to examine said manuscripts*," and to see that "they were his own compositions," not *hers*, which *she* "had left with him many years ago."

Now Mrs. Mary Baker G. Eddy, author of *Science and Health*, filled with "immortal mind" and the only "divine science" ever "demonstrated," is of course an honest woman. Many delightful innocents of all sizes would take her word for anything she promised. There is not a single member of her Church-Scientist who is not sure that her little hatchet is infinitely cleaner and brighter than George Washington's. Still, the possessors of the Quimby manuscripts, not yet having teetered themselves above all "earthly wisdom," would rather not trust her with their property.

A few years ago, the eldest of Dr. Quimby's two devoted friends, the Ware sisters, passed away. With the younger sister she left the following statement, in the form of an affidavit, which is here printed with permission:

"I, Emma G. Ware, of Portland, Maine, in the United States of America, do hereby declare that I knew personally the late Phineas Parkhurst Quimby, and that I and my sister, Mrs. Mackay (formerly Sarah E. Ware), were his patients while he resided in Portland, between the years 1859 and 1865, and that we both owe our restored health to his treatment or mode of teaching. I have learned that attempts are being made to deprive him of the credit of being the first to introduce the method of healing through the mind (or, more correctly, of applying moral philosophy to the cure of diseases), and I make this declaration out of regard to him, in order that the credit to which he is entitled may not, without protest, be assumed by others. I know that while Mr. Quimby resided in Portland he wrote out his ideas on Mental Science: he was not a scholarly man, and on that account copies of his writings were made by my sister, myself, and by Mr. Quimby's son, George A. Quimby. These copies were read over to Mr. Quimby, and such corrections made as he thought fit. They are now in the possession of Mr. George A. Quimby, who resides in Belfast, Maine, and my sister and I have also copies of a number of them. Beyond these, there are no other copies of his writings, if I except a few fugitive pieces which he gave away while he resided in Portland. The mode of reasoning pursued by Mr. Quimby is not new, but its application to disease as a remedy has not, so far as I am aware, been previously made in modern times. His teaching may be thus summarized: that all diseases, whether mental or physical, are caused by an error in reasoning, and that correcting the error will remove the cause, and restore the sufferer to health."

CHAPTER IV.
A GREAT "METAPHYSICAL" NOVEL.

As shown by our last chapter, Mrs. Mary Baker Glover Eddy, whatever divine attributes may have perched upon her, has been endowed with some very human qualities. But in one gift she has been strangely lacking—a good memory. For, in spite of her association with Dr. P. P. Quimby, his renovation of her broken system, and all the mellifluous prose and poetry she devoted to him in his day, the fruitful "mother," "discoverer," and "founder" of "Christian Science," when she came to set up her new religion, entirely forgot that her old friend, Quimby, was the real suggestion of her whole Shekinah. She not only failed to mention the fact, but she has been so miraculously forgetful, ever since, as to repudiate her own record of it, and to attempt the obliteration of it from sacred and profane history.

Mother Eddy's lack of memory, however, has had its plenary compensation. Her imagination has more than made up for it. The surcharge of this illimitable faculty has enabled her to produce one of the greatest works of fiction ever conceived on earth, or possible to any other planet. This arch-angelic romance, dimly and very distantly founded on fact, bears the esoteric title of *Retrospection and Introspection*. It is not in the usual form of a novel, but was evaporated by Mrs. Eddy as her corporal and spiritual biography, after she had dropped Dr. Quimby from her powers of research, and had built up her grand theological and financial industry, "Christian Science." From an attentive reading of this personally conducted and authorized volume, we know the light in which the hallowed lady wishes to appear, and we know a good deal more if we read between the lines.

At eight years of age—if we can only credit true piety hitched up with lost memory—a heaven-selected little girl, Mary Baker, "repeatedly heard a voice," calling her "distinctly by name, three times in an ascending scale." At first she thought it was a human voice; but in due season—for the call came many times— she, her mother and her cousin, Mehitable Huntoon, learned better. Then her mother read to her the Hebrew story of little Samuel, and advised her to respond to the voice, saying, "Speak, Lord, for thy servant heareth." Finally the chosen virgin took this advice, whereupon the voice "came no more" to her "*material* senses." Its mission had been fulfilled.

Such is the opening legend told to the marines of the Church Scientist, in that juicy book, *Retrospection and Introspection*.[17]

---

[17] *Retrospection and Introspection*, by Mary Baker G. Eddy, 10th thousand, 1896. Pages 7, 8, 9.

Still, in these days of "Spiritual manifestations," the numerous believers in messages from "the summer land" would account, in a quite simple way, for the voices calling little Hebrew Samuel and little New-England Mary. But not so Mrs. Mary Baker G. Eddy. "Am I a believer in Spiritualism?" she asks. "I believe in no ism.... As I understand it Spiritualism is the antipode of Christian Science."[18]

Ah, it was no voice of common, finite spirit, that came to the high and mighty founder of an "absolutely scientific religion." So there is but one conclusion she gives us to draw: *the voice was directly the voice of God*. The Infinite and Omniscient, the All-in-All, spake to the girl of nine years, as a miraculous call to her divine work. At that time, she tells us, her father thought her "brain" was "too large for her body."[19] The old gentleman was doubtless right. It looks, too, as if the brain of his blessed daughter, with the entire head containing it, has been rapidly enlarging ever since.

From the metaphysical adventures of Saint Mary Baker, as told in her *Retrospection and Introspection*,[20] we find that when twelve years old she was admitted to the "Orthodox Church" of New England, though she declined to accept the doctrine of predestination—a doctrine which so troubled her that a doctor was called, who pronounced her "stricken with fever." It is told of Martin Luther that when a theological student once came to him half-crazy over the same doctrine, the doughty reformer ordered him to go and get "well drunk." In the case of Robert Ingersoll, his soul could only find relief from the tenet by such hard swearing that it brought him peace. But we are assured by our divine lady of the "Church Scientist" that she took the better as well as the usual course prescribed for such trials. She "wrestled in prayer." For she felt sure that the Creator of the Universe, who had once descended in person and spoken to her by name, could not fail to possess the faculty of hearing and the usefulness of help. Behold it was so! Instantly the fever was gone and health was restored. "The physician marveled," she says, and John Calvin "lost his power."

In 1878 Rev. Mary Baker G. Eddy was called to preach at the Baptist Tabernacle of Boston. The congregation increased beyond the capacity of the pews, and it was no uncommon occurrence for the sick to be healed by her sermons. Cancers were cured, and "many pale cripples went into the church, leaning on crutches, who went out carrying them on their shoulders." Mrs. Eddy says so.[21]

By the same authority—in her *Retrospection and Introspection*—it is stated that her "Science of Divine Metaphysical Healing," otherwise "Christian Science," was "discovered" by her in 1866. The day and date are not given. But it was some time after February 15th; for at that time one Mary M. Patterson was occupied in putting on poetic mourning for Dr. P. P. Quimby, and in begging Mr. Julius A. Dresser to visit Lynn and heal an injury to her back from a fall on the ice.

It is not well to wear mourning too long. In the spring of 1866 it must have occurred to Mrs. Eddy that weeds of poetry would not pay, and she hustled them

[18] Ibid., page 35.
[19] *Retrospection and Introspection*, p. 10.
[20] Ibid., Page 12.
[21] The Great Novel, p. 17.

off. Dr. Quimby having gone "to heaven" and slipped out of a decayed memory, his obituary poetess just then realized that she had spent "twenty years" in tracing "physical effects to a mental cause." Then came the "scientific certainty" that "all causation" is "Mind," and that "every effect is a mental phenomenon."[22]

What "Christian Scientists" mean by "scientific certainty" is proof by "healing." Take the revered principle of cosmogony that "the moon is made of green cheese." If one who holds the doctrine, "heals" anybody, the proposition is "demonstrated." Mrs. Eddy's "scientific works" are all filled with this unanswerable logic. "Mortal Mind"—a thing which she utterly reprobates—may find difficulty in accepting the conclusion; but it is doubtless quite as well founded as most of the "healing" itself.

Mrs. Eddy's own case is an illustration in point. A bed-ridden invalid for years, she was snatched from death, she has told us, by Dr. Quimby, and within a week of his first mental treatment she climbed to the top of a city hall. The writer has read a series of Mrs. Eddy's unpublished letters, which show that for some time she had varied nervous and spinal relapses. When not with Dr. Quimby, she wrote to him for "absent treatments," and sometimes *saw him appear to her*—or said she did—in response. Finally she was cured. Then she fell on an icy sidewalk, was nearly frightened to death, and wrote her letter beseeching Mr. Dresser to "undertake" for her. But, having been taught mind-healing by Dr. Quimby, she "demonstrated" over herself, and got up. The Doctor's original cure appears to have been so effective that her fall on the ice was mostly a jar of her imagination and a contusion on her veracity. For, in her *Retrospection and Introspection*, she solemnly affirms that her accident caused an injury far beyond the reach of "medicine" or "surgery," which she repaired by application of the Divine Spirit. This experience, says Mrs. Eddy ("scientist"), was a "falling apple of discovery" to her. Thereupon she went out into the wilderness of Boston—"withdrew," that is, from society—for three years—that she might search the Scriptures and find "Science."[23] At the end of her retirement, she had learned that "Mind reconstructs the body," and that "nothing else can." How it is done, she adds, "the Spiritual Science of Mind must reveal." Her charge for a course of ten lessons in this "divine science" was soon fixed at "only three hundred dollars."[24]

Of the genuine original "Christian Science"—the sole and undivided "discovery" of Mrs. Mary Baker G. Eddy—she says:

"I named it *Christian* because it is compassionate, helpful, and spiritual. God I called *Immortal Mind*. That which sins, suffers, and dies, I named *mortal mind*. The physical senses, or sensuous nature, I called *error* and *shadow*. Soul I denominated *Substance*, because Soul alone is truly substantial. God I characterized as individual entity, but his corporeality I denied. The Real I claimed as eternal; and its antipodes, or the temporal, I described as unreal. Spirit I called the *reality*; and matter, the *unreality*."[25]

---

[22] *Retrospection and Introspection*, p. 28 to p. 35.
[23] The holy romance, page 28 and rest of chapter.
[24] *Retrospection and Introspection*, page 61.
[25] *Retrospection and Introspection*, p. 29.

On the hash and rehash of theology, here announced, we need not dwell just now, but will consider, for the moment, how much of Mrs. Eddy's individually discovered and copyrighted creed was first expounded, though *not* copyrighted, by one P. P. Quimby.

Dr. Quimby never thought of pushing his thought and work under the special name of "Christian Science," though his writings show that he used the term.[26]

He was not in pursuit of money by truckling to current preconception or prejudice. We recollect, however—for our own memory has not been laid in the tomb of our piety—that after "his truth was discovered" he "found his new views all portrayed and illustrated in Christ's teachings." We recollect that he said of his practise, "It belongs to a Wisdom that is above man as man. It was taught eighteen hundred years ago, and has never had a place in the heart of man since." He said, "There is a bread which, if a man eat, he is filled; and this bread is Christ or Science." In 1865 the Portland *Advertiser* said of Dr. Quimby:

"By a method entirely novel and at first sight quite unintelligible, he has been slowly developing what he calls *the 'Science of Health'*; that is, as he defines it, a science founded on principles that can be taught and practised like that of mathematics, and not on opinion or experiments of any kind whatsoever."

Prior to the issue of Mrs. Eddy's *Retrospection and Introspection* she had, of course, written her other great and better-known work of religious fiction, called *Science and Health*. Now the title of that book—the term "Science and Health"—is quite different from Dr. Quimby's term, "The Science of Health." Still, the chief distinction between them, considering what Dr. Quimby taught, is that the latter came first and the former afterwards.

It does not appear that God—who in our day has been personally known by Mrs. Eddy only—and in an interview which *He* took the trouble to seek—was ever technically defined by Dr. Quimby as "Immortal Mind," or "characterized as individual entity," with "corporeality denied." It may have been so; for all the obligations derived by Mrs. Eddy from Dr. Quimby have not yet been published. By all competent theologians and metaphysicians, since the beginning at least of human records, God has been conceived and proclaimed as Infinite Spirit, one with "Immortal Mind," and above "corporeality," which has been accounted a temporary phase of finite things. Plato was pretty nearly made of this conception in philosophy, and St. John in religion. P. P. Quimby was neither a Plato nor a Saint John; but he "agreed" with them, in his literal, honest fashion, as he said he did with Bishop Berkeley.

If Mrs. Eddy had ever read a history of philosophy before she instituted a religion, she would have found that Spinoza honored her advent, some two hundred years in advance of it, by postulating "Substance" as the "Soul" of things. Incidentally, too, he postulated "matter" as an "unreality of sense," and thus, in a way, as

____

[26] I have seen a brief article of his, entitled "Aristocracy and Democracy," and written under date of February, 1863, in which he said: "The religion of Christ is shown in the progress of Christian Science, while the religion of society decays in proportion as liberal principles are developed."—G. C.

"error" and "shadow" — the product of "mortal mind." Dr. Quimby said, with the utmost possible distinctness, "I believe matter to be nothing but an idea belonging to the senses"; and it will be found, when his writings get published, that he said the same thing in some hundreds of different ways. But all this was known to the thought of India, even before books were written, and the original authorities for it had then been lost.

But now: in one point of doctrine — and to her the most important one — Mother Mary Baker G. Eddy does stand completely "original," solitary and alone. She holds of "matter" that it is not only not what it seems, but is *nothing at all* save "unreality." To recognize it as anything whatever, beyond "shadow" and "error," is to be buried in disease, sin, and death. Absolutely to deny the most palpable fact of daily existence is to Christian Science the one road to health and salvation.

To Dr. Quimby, matter was a state of things "reduced from mind," but the state and the things were *here*. They were perfectly *actual* as *a condition*, though not as an unrelated fixture of all time and eternity. Every "idealist," in every age, has taken this view, excepting only Mrs. Eddy. Of her own view, no human being out of a refuge for imbeciles or the Church Scientist, could possibly begrudge her the sole copyright. In due order Mrs. Eddy's theological speculation will be further considered.

From the Arabian Nights tales of *Retrospection and Introspection*, we learn that, before setting up her new church, the revelator "wandered through the dim mazes of *Materia Medica*." She "found," in Jahr's two hundred and sixty-two remedies, the one pervading secret that the less matter and the more mind, the better the work. Homeopathy taught her that in the higher attenuations of its drugs, "matter is rarefied to its fatal essence, mortal mind." Her conclusion was that "mortal belief," instead of any "drug," governs the action of material medicine. "I claim," says she, "for healing scientifically," that "it does away with all material medicine, and recognizes the antidote for all sickness, as well as sin, in the Immortal Mind; and mortal mind as the source of all ills which befall mortals.... The mortal body being but the objective state of the mortal mind, this mind must be renovated to improve the body."[27]

Considering the high moral perch on which Mrs. Eddy has set herself, and contemplating the cerulean nest in which she has laid the eggs of "science," it is really painful here to study her case of fatty degeneration of the memory. For, apart from mere phraseology and acquaintance with Jahr, Dr. P. P. Quimby had reached the principle and practise of "healing scientifically," more than twenty years before she proclaimed it in *Science and Health*, and he had applied it to Mrs. Eddy herself, thirteen years prior to that publication, which descended from heaven in 1875. He did not mention "mortal mind" — by name, that is — for he called the fact of it "opinion of the natural man," in "the state of matter," and so far of "error." He did not use the term, "Immortal Mind"; for he designated it as "Wisdom," "Science," and the "Christ," as distinguished from "the man, Jesus." Adopting the Christ *principle*, Dr. Quimby aimed to follow, persistently but humbly, in the footsteps of Jesus. Dr. Quimby, in fact, was covering, both theoretically and practically, the

[27] *Retrospection and Introspection*, from p. 40 to p. 43.

whole true and essential field of "Christian Science," while avoiding its nonsense and its humbugs, at a time when Mrs. Eddy, as "Mary B. Glover," was a writer of love stories for "Peterson's Magazine."[28]

---

[28] This was half a century ago; but the productions—not "scribblings," of course, like Dr. Quimby's writings—are yet in mind among Mrs. Eddy's old acquaintances. One critic of them has said: "They were stories wherein the 'feller' married the girl in the last chapter, and they lived happily ever after except when the baby was cutting teeth. The stories were not essays, were not metaphysical, and were hardly physical. Had Mrs. Eddy not written them, I never should have remembered them at all."

CHAPTER V.

A SOFT SET OF CRITICS.

We have now learned a little of Mrs. Mary Baker G. Eddy's celestial and terrestrial biography, as derived from the supramundane novel, *Retrospection and Introspection*, and some other sources. Bare allusion has been made to her *Science and Health*. But this, she says, "is my most important work, containing the complete statement of Christian Science."

The book, as we have seen, came among men—or, more strictly speaking, among less busy women—in 1875; and a thousand copies, we are told, comprised the first edition. "The critics," Mrs. Eddy informs us, pronounced it "wholly original," but a thing that would "never be read."

The foolish "critics"! How little they knew about "originality"! But they knew still less of Mrs. Eddy's "Spiritual *afflatus*," as she designates it, in the fervency of which "erudite systems of philosophy" had "melted"; nor did they realize her "divinely appointed mission"; for, in 1891, *Science and Health* had reached sixty-two editions. "Then the critics said" that "Bishop Berkeley, David Hume, Ralph Waldo Emerson, or certain German philosophers," had originated Mrs. Eddy's sole and well-monopolized "Science."[29]

Now if any "critics" ever did really shoot such soft intellectual putty as that, they ought certainly to have been condemned to the most heroic sort of mind-healing.

Think of George Berkeley, the most acute, the most logical mind of his age, standing with both feet on John Locke's "Essay of the Human Understanding," and attempting to pull himself up into the Infinite by mouthing the shibboleth that there is no finite!

And David Hume—the bonny skeptic, David—whose keenness brought the philosophy of his age to a logical standstill, and for the moment broke up all "metaphysics"! Poor David Hume! In the hands of what a "critic" it was, who imagined he had ever furnished a speck of meat for such a haggis as *Science and Health*!

For the moment, let us pass by Mr. Emerson, the Puritan mystic of New England transcendentalism, who beamed serenely down on mere "critics," and told them he hoped he "had never said anything that needed to be proved." But Mrs. Eddy's phrase, "*certain German philosophers*," is one that can only refer to Immanuel Kant, with his school of followers, who summed up the pure thinking of the

---

[29] *Retrospection and Introspection*, p. 38 to p. 46.

modern world, as Plato and Aristotle summed up the pure thinking of the ancient world.

History tells us that Kant was a man who discovered the planet Uranus by mathematics before Herschel found it with a telescope, and who "had mastered all sciences" to date when he lived. Ripe with the knowledge of sixty years, he wrote his *Critique of Pure Reason*. This, the most profound and far-reaching treatise of any age, should have been named "The Analysis of Mind and Matter, Time and Space"; for such was really Kant's subject and achievement.

This extraordinary little German professor, Immanuel Kant, was the most regular and temperate of human beings; but he had a touch of asthma, for which, before all the medicinal properties of mind-cure were known, he took daily about a thimble-full of rum. Kant has been frightfully dealt with by his "critics," the most of whose heads he completely pulverized in connection with their activity in his behalf. But suppose Herr Professor Kant could have imagined that any "critic" on earth would ever accuse him of instigating the philosophy of Mary Baker G. Eddy! In that dread event, "the sage of Königsberg," who once lost the thread of a lecture when a button he used to finger was cut from his coat, might have been so disconcerted, so sunk in amazement and despair, as to swallow his whole bottle of liquor, instead of the twentieth of a gill, and to burn his *Critique of Pure Reason* in a fit of *delirium tremens*.

It is well he was tempted into no such catastrophe; for, on getting on a bit, we shall find that every possible system of "metaphysics," to have any scientific foundation in modern thought, must refer itself to Kant's dissection of the universe.

CHAPTER VI.

"THE PRECIOUS VOLUME."

In the world of books, Mrs. Eddy's *Science and Health* is the specially "precious volume"; for she herself so designates and describes it at the head of a chapter in her *Retrospection and Introspection*.[30] To her, indeed, it is a very precious volume—more precious than even a goodly pile of "the precious metals." Her devotees exchange these for it with sublime certainty that they get more than the worth of their money; and being in great need of science, to say nothing of health, their profuseness may be forgiven.

But it should be said at once that "Christian Scientists" are neither a bad nor a specially crude sort of the world's queer inhabitants. They are fanatically honest; and, as a whole, they have just that "little knowledge" which has long been proverbial as "a dangerous thing." Then they are quite incapable of looking through the veil worn by their beatific "Mother."

In the eyes of the unregenerate, these children of hers frequently turn to *Science and Health*, or to a picture of its author celestially touched up, when it would be well to inspect their plumbing and wash their windows. But this is no broad case against them; for almost any sort of camp-meeting, without regard to sect, is apt to bring upon the wicked some small inconveniences.

As can readily be seen, Mrs. Eddy's lambs are often amusing, and thus brighten life for less spiritual beings.

There is my babe-eyed friend, Mr. Tott. He never committed a cent's worth of sin in his life. He is a veritable piece of the salt of the earth, a little over-salted. But his youth has departed, and his sight is failing. He used to wear glasses; but he discarded them for "Christian Science" and a dim, economic light. He sees a little yet, though chiefly with "the eye of the mind." With this eye, however, he beholds marvels of "healing" going on all around him, which he proclaims and verifies at the weekly meetings of his church. He buys all Mrs. Eddy's books and publications, as fast as they come out. By patient effort he deciphers something of their contents. Then, as he contemplates an assertive text from *Science and Health*, or some tale of Jonah interpreted by Mother Eddy's *Key to the Scriptures*, a celestial calm descends on his soul, and folds it in a fabric softer than silk. He knows that he is better in health than ever before, that he sees better, and that the entire universe is becoming unspeakably illuminated. Disease never touches his physical frame; he has merely "a *belief* of a cold," or "a *belief* of a corn." In the etherialized Mr. Tott

---

[30] Page 45.

only one thing ever suggests a remnant of "wicked matter." Cast a doubt on the sainthood of Mrs. Eddy, then you behold an angel in anger. He may not indulge in personal violence, but he swiftly threatens that, if once you breathe your unholy doubt aloud, "Judge Hanna," or some other Sampson of "Science," will reduce you to a grease-spot.[31]

But, among all Mrs. Eddy's followers, her "precious volume," *Science and Health*, is paramountly precious to those who have paid their three hundred dollars for imbibing the inmost knowledge of her "unfathomable" religion, and have gone forth among the gentiles to teach and to heal. To a missionary "in science," the "precious volume" cannot be too preciously bound. Let the daintiest white of the white-winged dove encase its "inspired words," printed on translated tissue of ethereal linen. Let the sheen of the gold standard furnish splendor for the edges of the leaves, and letters for the cover. Let the book be held before the eyes of a new student or patient, with abysmal solemnity and mystic silence. Hypnotism, if you *name* it such, is bitterly disallowed; but "the precious volume" is so hallowed a thing that no danger can come from using it in the same way as the disk of a mesmerist. Impressiveness is the point—that self may depart, and "science" become boundless. Almost every religious sect in all history has had its fetich. "Christian Science" is not behind the procession. Mrs. Eddy's *Science and Health* is the fetich thereof. In a plain garment, for the poorer saints, it may be had for three dollars and eighteen cents. In the purest, holiest, most golden robe it costs six dollars.[32]

Let us look into *Science and Health* and see what it is; though the author warns us that something more than "mortal mind" is required to understand it. This she asserts and repeats with the voice, as it were, of a fog-horn grown eternal, until a multitude of people have come to think that the sound really contains significance. In her *Retrospection and Introspection* Our Lady of "The Precious Volume" says:[33]

"*Science and Health* is the textbook of Christian Science.... When the demand for this book increased, and people were healed by simply reading it, the copyright was infringed. I entered a suit at law, and my copyright was protected."

The case of "protected copyright" to which Mrs. Eddy refers, took place in 1883. A Mr. Arens had practised some sort of "mental healing," without the consent of the papal mother of "Christian Science." In connection with such healing he had issued some pamphlets, in which, according to the court records, he certainly came very near to reproducing certain sentences from *Science and Health*, which had a commercial value in his line, though they would not have sold for a cent out of "Science." The man's defense was that Mrs. Eddy's own works were not original with her, but had been copied from writings by Dr. Quimby.

Now Dr. Quimby, as we have seen, had sown the seed of the whole modern field of "mental healing," and Mrs. Eddy, as Mary M. Patterson, had told the whole truth about it. But Quimby's simple doctrine was that matter is a phase of mind;

[31] "Judge Hanna" is Mrs. Eddy's literary factotum. Mr. Tott is an actual personage, but, being "in Science," he will probably never recognize his picture—especially as there are many like him.

[32] See advertisements in all Christian Science publications.

[33] Page 47.

and hence that the mind of man, as an inlet of God's truth and power, can change the body and cure disease. Appropriating this thought, Mrs. Eddy had stretched it out and blown it up into the ponderous misfit labeled "Christian Science."

In 1883 none of Dr. Quimby's writings had been published, and there was no convenient evidence to prove that Mrs. Eddy had ascribed his mind-healing to "the Christ that was in him," and to his establishment of "Truth" in wrong-think-ing sick patients. As no such facts were presented, and as Mr. Arens had clearly plagiarized Mrs. Eddy, whatever *she* had done, the court properly decided that her "copyright" be "protected." In other words, the merits of the case were not involved, though the decision has given Mother Eddy a chance to say, with her usual candor and logic, that the failure of Arens "to produce his proof is *conclusive evidence* that *no such proof existed.*"

Science and Health is a book of nearly seven hundred pages, containing some-what less than two hundred thousand words; but this brief of Un-Christian Non-Science includes Mrs. Eddy's *Key to the Scriptures.*

The eighty-second edition of "the precious volume" is the particular issue here elucidated. We shall make a few quotations from *Science and Health*, but only just enough to verify our criticism of it as a pretentious, untrue, and unhealthy book, which, in the interest of the public, needs to be exploded. For these quotations we shall give Mrs. Mary Baker G. Eddy full credit. It would be a crime, indeed, to ac-cuse any one else of originating such capsules of metaphysical ipecac.

As laid down in *Science and Health*, the fundamental propositions of the mum-bo-jumbo termed "Christian Science" are four in number.

First: God is All.

Second: God is Good. Good is Mind.

Third: God, Spirit, being All, nothing is matter.

Fourth: Life, God, omnipotent Good, deny death, evil, sin, disease. Disease, sin, evil, death, deny Good, omnipotent God, life.

Mrs. Eddy says that, *to her*, these are *"self-evident* propositions." They are proved, too, by "the rule of inversion." They are just as harmonious backward as forward. There is a little hitch in Number Four, which declares one way that God denies death, evil, sin, and disease, and the other way that these deny God. But this one exception to "the rule of inversion" only confirms it; for, according to Scripture, God is true, and "every [mortal] man a liar."

For the corner-stone, then, of Eddyism, we have self-evident propositions—self-evident to the mind of Mrs. Mary Baker G. Eddy—and with these an appeal to Scripture. Truly enough this must be "Divine Science"; for no rational creature of modern times can suspect it of being human science, whether true or false. But, says the great teacher of it, "no human pen or tongue taught me the science," and "neither tongue nor pen can overthrow it." Well, never mind the overthrow. But, when Mrs. Eddy tells us that "no human pen or tongue" taught her "the science of mind-healing," we are obliged to infer that Dr. Quimby was more than human. How greatly would the plain but gifted Quimby have been shocked, had he foreknown that Mrs. Eddy would thus apotheosize him.

Through *Science and Health* we learn that "Christian Science" reveals, "incontrovertibly," that "Mind is All-in-all"—the only "realities" being "the divine Mind and idea." We learn, further, that this divine Mind is God, that God's idea is Man, and that by authority of Webster an "idea" is "an image in mind."

It would be truly pitiable for any theologian, or indeed for any believer in a spirit-principle of the cosmos, to attempt the "overthrow" of these venerable "revelations" now protected by Mrs. Eddy's copyright, but which were hoary with age even in the days of the Greek Academy. Barring Webster's definition of an idea, these "revelations" to Mrs. Eddy appear revealed in the Bible, though not copyrighted. As logical metaphysics, in recent times, Hegel reduced them to their utmost sublimation; and Hegel is excellent authority in many of our colleges, as well as with the good Dr. Harris, our United States Commissioner of Education at Washington.

Let us say once more that there is no trouble in effecting a spiritual derivation of the universe, except to our friends, "the materialists," who have themselves refined "matter" to things not much like it. The only trouble with an all-containing, all-pervading Spiritual Source of Existence, is in the funny havoc sometimes made of it by half-baked people, like "Christian Scientists."

To Dr. Quimby, "Mind," or "Spirit" was the principle of all things. To him, Matter was a condition of Spirit—"an idea," he said, "reduced to a solid"—a "solid" meaning a definite and real appearance to human sense. But this conception, which the old and regular school of metaphysicians have held for thousands of years, would not do for the genuine original "Mother of Christian Science" when she came to prescribe a dogma for the cure of all possible disease from leprosy to bunions. It was necessary, she thought, to have a stronger pill. She compounded it in the form that "matter," including the "mortal body," is not only "the objective state of the mortal mind," but that mortal mind is unmixed, "error," entailing all sin, disease, and death. Yet "error" is really "nothing"; or say something only to be *denied*. The duty of life, *"in Science,"* is to make this denial effective. Matter, sin, disease, are absolute illusions and delusions of "mortal mind," which itself is just "error," to be wiped out. Now say so, and they are all gone. Or if they persist in seeming to be anywhere, be more firm with them. Sing the denial, as well as say it. Keep it up. Let nothing else intervene for a second. Let every paragraph you write be made of it. Give it ten thousand different forms, and each form ten thousand variations. If you fully concentrate your whole mind on this "divine" business, and pay the full price for learning it, you will elevate yourself into "perfect harmony" with "Immortal Mind." When you accomplish this undertaking, impurity and evil, sin, disease and death, will disappear as the shadow of their original nothingness, which they always are and ever were.

Here is the whole real substance of "the precious volume," *Science and Health*, including Mrs. Eddy's marvelous *Key to the Scriptures*. Still, the holy tome has some interesting particulars.

On opening it, and journeying only as far as page 2, one finds that, while

"Christian Science" is copyrighted property, "the Divine Spirit" was the real author of it; for Mrs. Eddy explicitly declares that through "Christian Science" the Divine Spirit testified to her, and that the testimony unfolded her one basic, forever-echoed assumption that "matter" has nothing in it but "falsity."

Next comes up the Platonic conception—which, unfortunately for Plato, he neglected to copyright—that the Principle of Mind, with its reflection or "idea," constitutes the real universe. Mrs. Eddy pronounces this philosophical conception a scientific fact; but it was not "proved to the senses"—which, by the way, *never perceive anything but "error"*—until "Christian Science revealed it." Then it was proved "incontrovertibly, absolutely and divinely," by repairing Mrs. Eddy's back after a fall on ice.

From time immemorial, the history of philosophy has been familiar with the thought that the human body is a reflex and product of mind; a practical reality for all earthly conditions and purposes, but resolvable, from the view of spirit, into simply an objective appearance. The thought, too, has been frequent in poetry. Three hundred years ago Spenser sang:

> "So every spirit, as it is more pure,
> And hath in it the more of heavenly light,
> So it the fairer body doth procure
> To habit in, and it more fairly dight
> With cheerful grace and amiable sight.
> *For, of the soul, the body form doth take,*
> *For soul is form, and doth the body make.*

Yet Mrs. Eddy claims this doctrine, too, as her "discovery," though, with her, it is not merely "mind," but the "mortal" or "misnamed" article, that produces the body. All such "mind" is unalloyed "error," and the body, or apparition of this error, is another error. It was this "discovery," she says, that led to her infallible proposition, the all-inclusiveness of Immortal Mind and the all-nothingness of matter, which she made the bed-rock of her all-healing "Science."

Matter being Nothing, and our bodies being nothing but error, there is great use, notwithstanding, for the one genuine medicine, "Christian Science." "Physical healing," with "mental healing" thrown in, is the large wholesale business of which Mother Eddy is proprietor and director. In the last analysis, according to the preface of *Science and Health*, this medicine is "Divine Principle." Such a remedy naturally dispels the unfounded belief of matter, the unfounded imaginings of sickness and sin, which drop out of supposed reality, and so out of existence.

As the term "Christian Science" is necessarily suggestive of Christian history, even Mrs. Eddy has not quite claimed the whole product of Christianity as originating in *Science and Health*. She does admit, with pious candor, that God imparted the *spirit* of Christian Science to Jesus and the Apostles. But the *letter* is another thing. "The absolute letter" waited for Mary Baker G. Eddy; and, were the blessed lady a living kaleidoscope, she could hardly add to the combinations and varieties in which she presents this claim to her readers.

Eddyism proclaims One God, all-inclusive, whose highest title is "Immortal

Mind." But, "in Science," this God, being all-inclusive, as Unity, Identity, and Goodness—so otherwise all-*exclusive*—there is no room anywhere for a Devil, or say, rather, the *recognition* of one. If God is not only all, but all-good, no opposite to this principle can exist. However, there is "mortal mind," or "sense," with its image and creation, "matter," and in these are sin and disease. Still, mortal mind, matter, sin, disease, have no relation or reference to God. *He* "fills all Space."[34] *They* subsist neither by His creation nor permission. Hence they *can not be*—they are just *naught.*

But hold! Christian Science, with *Science and Health,* being present avatars to dispel sin and cure disease, such a science and such a book necessarily admit sickness and sin, both implicitly and explicitly. Now what is to be done in such a dilemma? Why, mortal mind, matter, evil, and all afflictions, while "nothing," are a kind of nothing that may be mentioned as "error" and ultimate "self-nullity." Thus, while Eddy Science, alias "Christian Science," has no real Devil, it has a very practical *seeming* Devil, and whips him from stump to stump with logic worse than himself. Finally, as he is not "substance," but "shadow," you knock him out by calling him names.

But the doctrine of the Trinity, as "demonstrated in Science," is the best abstract of the Eddy theology. This Trinity consists of one self-identical "Father-and-Mother God"; Man, "the Idea" or "Reflection"; then Christian Science, "the Holy Comforter."

The position of man, as theologized by Mrs. Eddy, is, if anything, more terribly mixed than that of the Devil. Man is "the image of God"; but, as God is *All,* man has "no real individuality." He cannot have personality of his own, as God has no "separability." Still this "God's idea," named man, somehow takes on an imaginary state, named "mortal mind," and this imaginary state has a dream of error and misery named "Sense." Human individuality, mortal mind, and sense, are all, in reality, null and void. Man, however, being God's idea and reflection, can never lose his unpossessed "true self." The divine contradictions of *Science and Health* are here insurmountable. Let no man try to rationalize them. Mrs. Eddy well remarks in her *Retrospection and Introspection,* that "Divine Science demands mighty wrestlings with mortal beliefs, as we sail into the eternal haven over the unfathomable sea of possibilities."

> O Lord, how long!
> Oh, bosh, how strong!

The fact is that any long-continued reading of *Science and Health,* with the innocence to imagine it either true, difficult or profound, is enough to turn a weak mind idiotic. To a trained thinker, the only danger from the book is an attack of nausea or a hemorrhage from laughing.

---

[34] This crude materialistic conception of "God" as "filling space" shows most beautifully the Kindergarten quality of Mother Eddy's "metaphysics."

CHAPTER VII.
"KEY" TO THE EDDY SCRIPTURE, SCIENCE AND HEALTH.

Mrs. Eddy's Un-Christian Non-Science may be summarized as a caricature of her early "New England Orthodoxy," crazily combined with New England Transcendentalism, coated with a kind of free-thought permissible only to her own "divine Science," all overlying Dr. Quimby's "Science of Health," and carefully put under copyright.

Let us now see a few moonstone gems from her "precious volume"—just enough to illustrate our criticism of it and not infringe on her monopolized territory.

It may be explained, by the way, that the United States statute governing copyright precludes the reproduction and sale of books and pamphlets, *as wholes*, without permission of the authors; and protects even *parts* of dramas, pictures, and other "works of art"—the intent being, of course, to protect, also, one of the Ten Commandments: "Thou shalt not steal." But, if an untrue and injurious book could not be analyzed, and a dozen extracts taken from it in proof of criticism, no literary quack could be exposed, in protection of the truth and the public. In that case, the Copyright Law would be worse than the old "Fugitive Slave Bill," and it would be a sacred duty to get into jail, if necessary, for violating it. Fortunately there is no such need. The law was not drawn in the interest of charlatans and malefactors, and has never been interpreted against the decencies of justice.

Following "Mother" Eddy's example in connection with our quotations from her *Science and Health*, we shall interpret them in a strictly "scientific" light, as she, with miraculous nerve, in her *Key to the Scriptures*, has done with other sacred writings. Thus we shall illumine *Science and Health* in the same way that she has illumined *Genesis* and *The Apocalypse*.

Science and Health, 7.[35]—"In the year 1866 I discovered the Science of Metaphysical Healing, and named it Christian Science. God had been graciously fitting me, during many years, for the reception of a final revelation of the absolute Principle of Scientific Mind-healing."

Interpretation "in Science."—History reveals to us, for sure, that "Mother Eddy," has always *claimed* to have discovered and founded the only genuine and original Christian Science. Though she was once a patient of Dr. P. P. Quimby, and at that

---

[35] The figures stand for the pages referred to.

time one Mary M. Patterson said that Quimby cured disease by mental truth—"the truth that Christ taught"—this miserable episode has nothing to do with the case. Mrs. Eddy has told us that the Patterson woman was a creature "ignorant" of "Science," whom Dr. Quimby used to "mesmerize." He cured her of a seven-years' complaint in the mortal body, but so addled her head that she had no knowledge of what she talked about. Thus, Mrs. Patterson's impression that Dr. Quimby was the modern founder of mind-healing has no weight. The truth was not in her. But Mother Eddy, notwithstanding she herself was once that same Mrs. Patterson, discovered all truth and all science, without regard to any of her previous statements.

Science and Health, 453.—"A Christian Scientist needs my work on Science and Health for his textbook, and so do all his students and patients.... It is the voice of Truth to this age, and contains the whole of Christian Science, or the Science of healing through Mind.... It was the first published book containing a statement of Christian Science.... It registered this revealed Truth, uncontaminated with human hypotheses. Other works, which have borrowed from this book without giving it credit, have adulterated the Science."

Interpretation "in Science."—It is evident that everybody "in Science" should buy its real Bible, *Science and Health*; for the Old and the New Testament, while it is policy to use them in the Church Scientist, are in dreadful need of exegesis by Mary Baker G. Eddy. She is the one religious person, altogether scientific, that now exists in the world. She is "uncontaminated truth," and anything that interferes with her abets larceny and spreads leprosy. Moreover, it is a financial crime against her, conducive to heart-disease. Let it again be stated that "the precious volume," *Science and Health*, is cheap for cash, ranging from only $3.18 to $6.

Science and Health, Pref. VIII.—"The question, What is Truth? is answered by demonstration—by healing disease and sin."

Interpretation "in Science."—That truth can only be set on its absolute end by curing megrims and other unhealthiness, has been incontrovertibly settled by the religious experience of "Mother Eddy" herself. When she rose into the revelation that matter is nothing—not even a phenomenal condition of anything—the truth instantly spliced her broken spine. It was this "demonstration by healing" that transformed the ignorant, deluded, mesmerized Mary M. Patterson, into our holy, scientific, infallible Lady of the "Precious Volume."

Science and Health, 2 and 3, passim.—"The divine Spirit, testifying through Christian Science, unfolded to me the demonstrable fact that matter possesses neither sensation nor life.... Human experiences show the falsity of all material things.... My discovery that erring, mortal, misnamed *mind*, produces all the organism and action of the mortal body, led up to my demonstration that Mind is All, and matter is naught, as the leading factor in Mind-Science.... The revelation of Truth in the understanding came to me gradually, and apparently through divine power. When a new spiritual idea is borne to earth, the prophetic Scripture of Isaiah is renewedly fulfilled: 'Unto us a child is born ... and his name shall be Wonderful.'"

Interpretation "in Science."—That there is absolutely nothing in anything you see, feel, hear, taste or smell, is eternally laid down as "the leading factor in Mind-Science." Though the ideas of Mrs. Mary Baker G. Eddy are all wonderful, this is the most surpassingly wonderful of all. But Mother Eddy herself is much more wonderful than even her ideas. As little Mary Baker she was wonderful in her likeness to little Samuel; as Mary M. Patterson, she was more wonderful as a mesmerized victim of Dr. Quimby; and, as Mary Baker G. Eddy, she is most wonderful, as the Ark of the Covenant of the only true Medicinal Religion. All Mother Eddy's writings point, all the time, to this beautiful lesson.

Science and Health, 5.—"No analogy exists between the vague hypotheses of Agnosticism, or Millenarianism, and the demonstrable truths of Christian Science; and I find the will, or sensuous reason of the human mind, to be opposed to the divine Mind, expressed through Divine Science."

Interpretation "in Science."—All the ancient and modern "isms," except Eddyism, we must sit on and blot out. The most of them are unpopular, and don't bring us in anything. But he who opposes Eddyism contradicts the Divine Mind, expressed through Divine Science, which, logically, must be the production of our Divine Mother.

Science and Health, 8.—"The phrase *mortal mind* implies something untrue, and, therefore, unreal."

Interpretation "in Science."—This truth is to be taken as infallible on all occasions. Still, the unreality, mortal mind, is a thing to be healed by Christian Science, and there is money in the metaphysical pills.

Science and Health, 21.—"There is no physical science, inasmuch, as all true Science proceeds from divine Intelligence."

Interpretation "in Science."—Shut up your arithmetic, geometry, physics, and astronomy. They amount to nothing. There is no truly scientific book except *Science and Health*.

Science and Health, 25.—"Must Christian Science come through the Christian churches, as some insist? This Science has come already, and come through the one whom God called."

Interpretation "in Science."—Christian Science, my beloved, is copyrighted property, and can only spread through the owner and her deputies. The "one whom God called" is Mrs. Mary Baker G. Eddy.

Science and Health, 244, 245, 473, 284.—"The act of describing disease makes the disease. Warning people against disease frightens them into it. This obnoxious habit ought to cease.... The unscientific practitioner says: 'You are ill; you must rest.' Science objects to all this.... Mind controls the body and brain.... A cup of tea is not the equal of Truth.... A material body is a mortal belief.... The medicine of Science is divine Mind."

Interpretation "in Science."—Your doctor is a fool, whether he be allopathic, homeopathic, magnetic, or even of any *unauthorized* school of mind-healing. Dismiss him, and send for a Christian Science M. D., authorized to practise by Mrs. Mary Baker G. Eddy. If he can't cure you, it will not be his fault; it will be simply because your mind, or the minds around you, or both, are out of tune with *Science and Health* and *its Key to the Scriptures.*

Science and Health, 259, 480, 475.—"Electricity, the offspring of finite mind, is unreal.... The physical universe expresses the conscious and unconscious thoughts of mortals. Physical force and mortal mind are one.... Matter is neither self-existent nor a product of Spirit. An image of mortal thought, reflected on the retina, is all the eye beholds."

Interpretation "in Science."—That a force like electricity has no reference to any principle or power but finite mind, will always be hard for an unscientized person to believe. But Mother Eddy knows, and her word must go. Still, the unreality of electricity is not quite so to people "out of science." If one toys with a trolley-wire before he has read and understood *Science and Health,* he may experience a slight shock of reality, if he lives long enough. But one who has purchased Mrs. Eddy's great work, and who reads it constantly, need have no fear of electrocution, or anything else. His mortal mind has pretty nearly departed from him. His "physical universe" is hardly a picture of "conscious thoughts," and his "unconscious thoughts," whatever such things may be, will never lead him into much danger.

Science and Health, 487.—"Science reveals material man as a dream at all times, and never as the real Being."

Interpretation "in Science."—Mortals are nothing. The One and Only Being is the Father-and-Mother God of Christian Science. Our Mother is Mrs. Mary Baker G. Eddy.

Science and Health, 411.—"The Scientist knows there can be no hereditary disease, since matter cannot transmit good or evil intelligence to man, and Mind produces no pain in matter."

Interpretation "in Science."—On the ground that mind and matter are absolutely unconnected, there can be no doubt of there being no hereditary disease. On the same ground there can be no heredity itself, and no world for heredity to exist in. How true it is, "in Science," that all actuality has no actuality in it!

Science and Health, 28.—"The true Logos is demonstrably Christian Science."

Interpretation "in Science."—We know, too, from Mrs. Eddy's "precious volume," that Christian Science, in addition to being the Logos, is the Holy Comforter. Thus her copyrighted religion is two-thirds of the Trinity.

Science and Health, 411.—"The daily ablutions of an infant are no more natural or necessary than would be the process of taking a fish out of water every day, and covering it with dirt, in order to make it thrive more vigorously thereafter in its native element.... Water is not the natural habitat of humanity."

Interpretation "in Science."—Don't take the trouble to wash the baby. His body is only an expression of mortal mind, and is thus so mussed up with error and nothingness that water will never get him clean. His proper habitat is "Science." Scrub his "conscious and unconscious thoughts" with Christian Science, and never mind the rest of him.

We shall make but one more quotation, here, from Mrs. Eddy's "Divine comedy," *Science and Health*. There is no use of being too serious with it. History will soon take it as mostly a "grim joke" on metaphysics, theology, and medicine. But one thing must give us pause. On approaching the Lord's Prayer, one feels himself on solemn ground, if such ground there be anywhere in life, and for once, if never before, puts on the mantle of conservatism. But, to Mrs. Eddy, the words of Jesus in devotion and supplication—at once the simplest and grandest words ever uttered—require her "spiritual interpretation." What, in her index to *Science and Health*, she terms the "Spiritualized version" of the Lord's Prayer is this:

"Our Father and Mother God, all-harmonized, Adorable One. Ever present and Omnipotent. Thy Supremacy appears as matter disappears. Give us grace for to-day; Thou fillest the famished affections; and Love is reflected in love. And leavest us not in temptation, but freest us from sin, disease and death; for Thou art all Substance, Life, Truth, and Love, forever.—*So be it.*"

The author of the *English Bards and Scotch Reviewers* tells of a poet who

"Breaks into blank the Gospel of St. Luke,
And boldly pilfers from the Pentateuch;
And, undisturbed by conscientious qualms,
Perverts the Prophets, and purloins the psalms."

Let any one not "in Science" ask himself if Mrs. Mary Baker Eddy has not gone farther and done worse.

CHAPTER VIII.

"CHRISTIAN-SCIENCE" ORGANIZING FORCES.

As Mrs. Eddy has been a manufacturer and vender of "Christian Science" for a comparatively short time—only a quarter of a century—many good people who knew her at the inception of that successful industry are still on earth, in an active condition of "mortal mind." They have volunteered to furnish for this brief book a variety of plain and ornamental information that is not essential to it. But, in justice to history and biography, one point must not be omitted. They all agree that "Mother Eddy," like Cæsar, the Standard Oil Company, and the Sugar Trust, has more organizing capacity than "the sons and daughters of God," to use her own phrase, generally possess. With this capacity, it is also agreed that never a Bonaparte, never a Jay Gould, never a Pierpont Morgan, could be more handy in surmounting all over-nice impediments to practical success.

Thus by her rare combination of terrestrial and celestial genius, "Mother Eddy" has been able to hold her copyrighted religion, "Christian Science," strictly under her personal regnancy, and direct it to the highest financial, doctrinal, and healing ends. She permits no tinge of private judgment, no stain of unauthorized opinion, and no mere finite criticism, so far as she can silence it. She is the Church, and membership is obedience. Hence she bitterly antagonizes all independent agencies of scientific salvation, though with eyes rolled up, and with fervent proclamations of unbounded "love." In her *Science and Health*, she advises her readers not to read other "scientific works," as they are full of "materialism," and are not "Scientifically Christian." Directly or indirectly, too, there is always the point that money can be much better invested in Mrs. Eddy's own "sacred" and "positively demonstrated" writings. It would almost seem that, in her universal motherhood, Mrs. Mary Baker G. Eddy must have borne Mohammed's great soldier who burned the Alexandrian library in devotion to the *Koran*.

To a great organizer, a wholesale business is always more attractive than retail trade. It is handled quite as easily, with less detail, and thousands of small merchants contribute to the proceeds. The able founder of "Christian Science" early realized this fact—in her case drawn from on high, but sometimes reached through commercial experience. Having retired into the wilderness of her mind, far from all monitions of "sense"; having trained her memory to forget the existence of "matter," "error," and Mary M. Patterson; having taken a three-years' vacation with her only peers, "the ancient worthies" and "the Scriptures"; Mrs. Eddy came back at last, among the human species, with the metaphysics and curative formulas of "Christian Science." Then came practical transactions in "revelations" and "mental medicine," which soon rivaled the sales of Mrs. Winslow's Soothing Syrup and Lydia Pinkham's celebrated compound.

Though Mrs. Eddy has gradually taken into her service various literary experts, theologico-commercial travelers and metaphysical auctioneers, she has always supervised, in person, the wholesale department of "Christian Science." On her return from the skies, she brought down a large collection of documents in which "the whole science" was condensed and canned, and all the medical prescriptions required to fulfil a millennium of holiness and health. With these documents in hand she formed classes of "loyal students," her definition of "loyalty" being "allegiance to God" (as manifested in Mary Baker); "subordination of the human" (the student) "to the divine" (the teacher); "steadfast justice" (no wobbling over the cash); and strict adherence to "divine Truth and Love" (the Mother of the Logos and the Holy Comforter forever glorified).

To be more specific, it was in the year 1867 that Mrs. Mary Baker Glover Patterson, freed by divorce from the last-named culprit, and married to Asa Gilbert Eddy, began, as she records it, the teaching of "Christian Science Mind Healing" to "one student." Here was a good seed sown in fructifying ground; for, in 1881, it had grown to be "The Massachusetts Metaphysical College" of Boston.[36]

This vast institution was managed by Mrs. Eddy as chief impartress of "science," her assistants being her husband, her adopted son, and a General Bates. These four "scientists" constituted the faculty.

Mrs. Eddy's last husband is described, by those who knew him, as one of the most humble and obedient men that ever blest a perfect woman in immaculate matrimony. His value as a college professor may be inferred from one reminiscence of him. His supreme better-half once sued a poor young doctor who had fallen away from "science," and taken to homeopathy, that she might collect her fee for having taught him "Christian Science therapeutics." Her husband, Asa, was a witness for her, to prove the pecuniary value of her instruction, and was asked, among other questions,

"What is Man?" "As near as I can make it out," replied Prof. Eddy, "Man is an image." Mrs. Eddy lost her case, as the court was too unspiritual to reduce her "metaphysics" to dollars and cents.[37] But the good Asa showed that he was an "image" of Mary; and, in her *Retrospection and Introspection*, she has gratefully embalmed his memory in a text from the Psalms.

"Mark the perfect *man*, and behold the upright: for the end of *that* man *is* peace."

The italics are not in the psalm, but are Mary's.

Some further conception of "the perfect man," Prof. Eddy, and the value of Mother Eddy's estimate of him, may be gathered from an item which appeared in the Boston *Evening Herald* of December 7, 1878, stating that "Edward J. Arens and Asa G. Eddy were indicted to-day by the Grand Jury for soliciting James H.

[36] *Retrospection and Introspection*, p. 51.

[37] These facts are well remembered and well recorded. They were of special interest to such of Mrs. Eddy's "loyal students" as had seceded from her cult. —G. C.

Sargent to kill Daniel H. Spofford." It appears that Spofford, in order to probe the matter, led on the conspiracy, and so became technically involved in it himself. Thus the affair became so mixed up that, according to the official court-record, the District Attorney concluded not to prosecute the indictment, and Arens and Eddy were "discharged *on payment of costs.*" The divine "Mother Eddy" surely could not have instigated a conspiracy to murder Spofford (a troublesome backslider from "Science"), though he and many other backsliders, who know her well, have long labored under the impression that the whole enterprise was hers.

The human head is a queer bulb, and often seems to be a direct evolution from the squash. This hypothesis, illustrated by the researches of Darwin and his school, accounts for the rapid growth of Mrs. Eddy's Massachusetts Metaphysical College from 1881 to 1889, when, in the latter year, she closed it. At that time, as she recollects things, her college was not only filled, but "flooded" with students from all parts of America, Europe, and the world. Three hundred applications were on the list, and the number was rapidly increasing.[38]

If Mrs. Eddy were not so far above the world and the flesh that her reasons for things seldom comport with a sub-lunar search into them, it might be possible to believe that she discontinued her college because she feared that "material organization," applied to "Christian Science," would obstruct "Love's Spiritual compact." Whatever it means, this at least is what she *says.* The success of her college had shown her the danger of placing people on "earthly pinnacles"; and even "mortal mind" can see that such a setting-up might lead students away from the primal Mother and the central contribution-box. Besides, she had always had "conscientious scruples" against "giving diplomas" when she thought of those same "earthly pinnacles."

It may throw some light on the sudden closing of "The Massachusetts Metaphysical College" to note that, notwithstanding "Mother" Eddy's "conscientious scruples" against granting mere "diplomas," she had issued hundreds of meta-physico-medical degrees at high prices.

According to a statement of hers, she obtained her college charter from the State of Massachusetts in 1881, "with the right to grant degrees." But the act on which this grant was based was repealed in 1882. Then, in 1883, the conferring of "any diploma or degree" by any "corporation" or "association," was made a legal offense, punishable by a fine of not less than $500. Being the "president," not of any "corporation" or "association," but of a regular "college" (with a faculty of three beside herself), Mother Eddy's legal mind has held that this law, if aimed at her, failed to hit, though it knocked out all other mind-healing colleges.[39] But, in 1889, when, as persistent rumor has it, the problem was about to be solved by legal process against "Mother Eddy," the subject was practically closed by the closing of her "college," and by her retirement to New Hampshire, where "the wicked cease from troubling and the weary are at rest."

Considering Mrs. Eddy's kind of "college-faculty" and "board," together with her exhaustive copyrights and the hierarchical monopolies consequent upon them,

[38] *Retrospection and Introspection*, p. 57.
[39] See *Christian Science History*, by Septimus J. Hanna, p. 42.

it is quite conceivable that when time was ripe she had no difficulty in "unanimously" passing resolutions to discontinue her "flourishing school." The little joker in this pack of resolutions soon came out in one of them. It deftly touched the matter of "organization," and then propounded that "the hour" had "come" when "the great need" was for "more of the Spirit," not "the letter," and that *Science and Health* was the spirit's nutriment.

It is not directly stated by Mother Eddy in this connection, that God Himself fixed the scale of prices for her book; but she does say it was "God" who "impelled" her to "set a price" for her "instruction in Christian-Science Mind-Healing." The price was three-hundred dollars a head, for a college course of three weeks. At first she "shrank from asking it." But "a strange providence" led Mary to these terms, and "God," she asserts, "has since shown" her, in "multitudinous ways," the "wisdom" of her "decision."[40] The "strange providence" and "the multitudinous ways" are not explained by her; but the "wisdom" of gathering together fat bank-deposits is unanimously acknowledged in the Church Scientist.

When our republic was a hundred years old, it had become worthy of having "The First Christian Science Association." That body was accordingly organized, on the fourth day of July, 1876, by Mrs. Eddy and six of her head-light reflectors. Three years later, the Association balloted on forming a Church, and the Eddyites won by a large plurality. Rev. Mary Baker G. Eddy was of course chosen its "first pastor," and during her ministration it prospered in numbers and popularity. That is, she says so in her *Retrospection and Introspection*. But owing to tons of work, which increased upon her, she was unable to give the Church sufficient attention, and no son or daughter of "Science" was competent to take her place. Her church was "envied" and "molested" by other churches, and there was danger of "Christian warfare"—which might have led to a diminution of proselytes, and more horrible still, a loss of shekels. In such an extremity, she "recommended" the dissolution of the First Church Scientist, and again, as ever, her recommendation went through "without a dissenting voice."

"This measure," she tells us, was followed by "a great revival" in the way of "mutual love," with "spiritual power" and "prosperity." Those, we may be sure, were money-making times. Mrs. Eddy's reasons for dissolving her church were doubtless infallible. Still, that same church at once resurrected itself and exalted its horn—the "Mother Church" in Boston, and then children and grandchildren galore, in hundreds of secondary "Hubs" and their suburbs.

---

[40] For this amazing snivel see *Retrospection and Introspection*, p. 61.

CHAPTER IX.

THE ONE TRUE "MOTHER CHURCH."[41]

It was in 1889, says Mrs. Eddy, that "I gave a lot of land in Boston," on which to erect "a church edifice" as "a temple for Christian Science worship."[42] The land, she is particular to say, was worth "twenty thousand dollars," and was "rising in value." As she has been careful to mention this increment of the "rise" —not hiding it under a bushel, but setting it on top of the cover—we must be sure to add it to the sum of the original benevolence.

But how much labor could be saved by a meek historian if only Mrs. Eddy's word could ever be safely accepted without looking behind it! On consulting the official registry of such matters, one finds that before Mrs. Eddy gave her land to the Church of Christ Scientist, *the Church itself owned the land*, under a mortgage of nine thousand dollars, four thousand of which had been paid off. The balance was five thousand. The provident "Mother" bought this mortgage and foreclosed it. She then conveyed the property to the trustees of the First Church of Christ Scientist, reserving the right to re-enter and repossess the land, with improvements, in case a church erected on it should not be run to suit her. All this was specified in ten conditions, which the angels have not recorded in her biography.

Adjoining the Eddy castle of "metaphysics" are two lots on which stand two buildings of the Christian Science Publishing Society. This real estate was set down in February, 1898, by the editor of "The Christian Science Journal," to be worth not less than twenty-two thousand dollars. On January 25th, 1898, "Mother" Eddy generously conveyed it to the First Church of Christ Scientist. *But,* three days before—on the 21st of January, 1898—the Christian Science Publishing Society, for the sum of one dollar, had *conveyed it to her*. The string tied to her *re*-conveyance was that she should "have and occupy so much room conveniently and pleasantly located" in the establishment, as might "be necessary to carry on the publication and sale" of her "books" and "literature" —a reservation of "room" which, under legal stress might easily be interpreted to mean the whole thing—it being distinctively a "publishing house."

With Mother Eddy's donation of January 25th, 1898, she threw in "The Christian Science Journal" and "all the literary publications of the Society" —these having been turned over to her with other things, for one dollar, on January 21st,

[41] This chapter is written mostly from personal inspection and knowledge. An elaborate description of the Church is given in The Christian Science Journal for January, 1895.— G. C.

[42] *Retrospection and Introspection,* page 62.

1898—she saving to herself "only the right to copyright the 'Journal' in her own name—an excellent way to make it self-supporting, with no liability on her part to incur its debts, while yet she could hold it under her absolute dictation.

"Let us endeavor," says the editor of "The Christian Science Journal" (February, 1898), "to lift up our hearts in thankfulness to God ... and to his servant, our Mother in Israel, for these evidences of a generosity and self-sacrifice that appeal to our deepest sense of gratitude, even while surpassing our comprehension."

Now such an evidence of generosity and self-sacrifice may intelligibly "surpass" the "comprehension" of any stipendary of Mrs. Eddy' paid to write such stuff as the foregoing; but Mary Baker Eddy's real bounty, generosity, self-sacrifice and benefaction, consisted in cancelling a mortgage of five thousand dollars, by which, on land thus obtained, a church costing other people two hundred and fifty thousand dollars was soon built to her glory, she keeping a Shylock grip on the land, church and the adjacent property of her functionaries, with all its appurtenances that were good for anything.

When "Mother Eddy" casts a loaf of bread upon the waters, it is always safe to look for a hundred loaves on the way back to her.

"The First Church Scientist"—the edifice erected on Mrs. Eddy's donation of land—is a handsome structure of rough granite, looking something like a small armory with a big tower. This sacred castle of "metaphysics" is situated a little on the outskirts of residential fashion in the Hub-City, the district thereof being the Back Bay. It is accessible to the world, when once in Boston, by "the electrics" and a short walk. As a place of scientifico-religious assemblage, the building seats twelve hundred actual "scientists" in the flesh, and the sympathetic spirits of some twelve thousand other "members," absent throughout the country. On this account, some Eddyites who have never seen it regard its size as rivaling that of the earth.

The Cathedral (scientist) has much stained glass, and on nearly every window is depicted some Mary; for all *good* Marys, particularly the Marys of the Bible, inferentially point to Mary Baker Eddy. This Mary's *Science and Health* is exceedingly prominent in the multi-colored glass, and so gives countenance to all the representations taken from the Scriptures.

An organ is prominent—a large, harmonious present from a gentleman who thinks that somebody was cured of something by Christian Science.

The church has two pretty pulpits side by side, from one of which the Bible is read, while from the other, that ancient book is kept straight by the reading of its only true meaning from *Science and Health*.

Singing the praises of "Immortal Mind," as discovered by Mrs. Eddy, constitutes a part of the services, but there is no preaching—which is just as well, perhaps, but needs a word of explanation.

Preaching used to be allowed "in Science"; but some of Mother Eddy's apostles, having just enough knowledge for their creed, yet great gifts of speech, sermonized, it is said, with such honest zeal that their eloquence was in danger of casting an unglorified shadow on the Mother herself. It must be stated, indeed, that sundry who have listened to St. Mary (scientist) affirm that her divine pen has always been much more potent than her divine tongue. And some go so far as to declare that her sermons, when she preached, were often dull to the non-elect, even if they cured every disease within ten miles of them. However these things may have been, Mrs. Eddy, early in 1895, issued the following ecclesiastical edict:[43]

"Humbly, and as I believe divinely directed, I hereby ordain that the Bible and *Science and Health* with *Key to the Scriptures* shall hereafter be the only pastor of the Church of Christ, Scientist, throughout our land, and in other lands."

This edict prevented Mrs. Eddy's theological subordinates from setting themselves up on "earthly pinnacles." Mother Eddy at the same time decreed this:

"No copies of my books are allowed to be written, and read from manuscript, either in private, or in public assemblies, except by their author."

She included the commandment that

"The reader of *Science and Health* with *Key to the Scriptures*, shall commence by announcing the full title of this book, with the name of the author, and afterwards repeat at each reading its abbreviated title."

Directions followed regarding classes in "Christian Science"—the number of pupils each teacher might instruct, and the annual number of classes—all to be taught "from the Christian Science text-book."

Thus "Mother" Eddy's edict of 1895, abolishing pulpiteers "in Science," while it redounded widely to her own glory, piously amplified, also, the proceeds of her "precious volume," *Science and Health*. But to the innocent lambkins of her church, she said:

"Teaching Christian Science shall be no question of money, but of morals and uplifting the race."

So that lovely bird, the ostrich, still buries her head in the sand, but leaves out much that ornaments the landscape.

In a rounded corner of the First Church Scientist, but conspicuous from the main passage, is a little apartment celebrated as "The Mother's Room." There is no use of mentioning the Mother Church "in Science," without dwelling on "The Mother's Room." It is never done, especially by any "Scientist." The Church is holy, throughout; but that room is the demonstrated environment of Immortal Mind.

The entrance to "The Mother's Room" is through a white-marble arch, lustrous to behold. Over the door, cut into the marble, is the inscription, "LOVE." It is not "love of money," or "love of flattery," but just "LOVE." On the floor of the entrance we read in mosaic: "Mother's Room. The children's offering"—which signifies that Mother Eddy knows how to attract the pennies of little Scientists as well as the dollars of her larger infants.

As you enter the room, you tread on white-marble mosaic, sprayed with figs

____

[43] Published in the *Christian Science Journal* of April, 1895.

and fig-leaves, and you feel an emanation of pale green and old rose. If you know your business, you are struck with awe on being in this holy-of-holies.

On your right is a mantel of white Italian marble and gold, with an open fire-place, wherein to throw all your mortal thoughts, that they may be consumed. Opposite the mantel on your left, is a rather large painting, set back in the wall, but well lighted by electricity and divine science. It shows the sacred chair in which Mrs. Eddy sat when she wrote *Science and Health*. The chair is empty—as typical, perhaps, of her departure from Boston when she closed her "Metaphysical College." As Mrs. Eddy has no need of a table when she writes, but can perform miracles of literature on a pad, the picture shows this phenomenon. Sheets of her manuscript are scattered on the floor, illustrating the logical chaos which fills them.

A part of "The Mother's Room" is fenced off by a ribbon, to protect a rug made from the downy breasts of five hundred eider-ducks. The legend, as told by the guide, is that "no man's hand ever touched this rug." It is sacred to the Mother's immaculate foot. But it was not manufactured by the Audubon Society.

A beautiful showcase, of white and gold, ornaments the room, and in it are the white and gold editions of Mrs. Eddy's works. They are samples of what you can buy at the regular price, and are very tempting to wealthy "scientists."

The Mother's room has a gorgeous bay-window, or three windows in one, of stained glass. The Mother herself is there, searching the Scriptures, encircled by a halo from the star of Bethlehem. The Christian Science seal is emblazoned on the window, and a little girl is there, reading *Science and Health* to an old man. The little girl must be Mary Baker and the old man, probably, is Moses or Abraham. An alabaster bee-hive must not be forgotten, which contains the names of the little busy bees "in Science"—those children who squeezed out the cash to construct the room.

As you turn and go out, you observe, on the right, an alcove, which contains a folding bed, to be pulled out into the main room in case of use; for the alcove itself is almost as small as a mind that disagrees with Mrs. Eddy.

At your left—still going out—there is a toilet-room, corresponding to the alcove, but on the other side of the arch and doorway. In practical construction, this toilet-room is very much like other small inclosures adapted to the same ends. The chief difference, here, is that all the water-pipes, faucets, and such fixtures, are plated with gold. Thus Mother Eddy's lavatory proudly reminds her of Solomon's temple at Jerusalem.

It is said that "Mother Eddy" has never slept in "The Mother's Room" but once. This one occasion, however, was quite enough to sanctify it forever.

CHAPTER X.

A MARTYR TO "SCIENCE."

"Christian Science," though its span be brief, has produced one of the most exceptional martyrs that ever lived and prospered. It is a woman, of course; for men, as a rule, have now become too "mortal-minded" for sacrificial victims.

The lady referred to is a Mrs. Josephine C. Woodbury. Boston is her habitat. She was long a follower of Rev. Mary Baker G. Eddy, and was a preacher of the gospel, *Science and Health*. She talked and prayed, she wrote and traveled, all "in Science," until she became a public personage, celebrated throughout the dominions of the Eddyites. Then at last there was "War in Heaven"—which is the title of one of Mrs. Woodbury's books,[44] and she was excommunicated from the Mother Church Scientist of the Boston Back Bay.

Now Mrs. Woodbury is not a lady who can be excommunicated from a church without giving that church fair returns for the outlay. Mrs. Woodbury has a pen, and there is black ink on it. She has attorneys quick to exchange legal process for bank notes redeemable in gold. The lady has turned her pen against "Mother Eddy," and cast ink-spots on the "Mother's" religion, not to say her personal character. The Woodbury lawyers have been let loose upon "the Mother" to sue for ethical redress and monetary damages.[45]

Mrs. Woodbury entered "Science" very young—a fact on account of which let us excuse her, as well as we can, for ever entering it at all. She thought she was one of the "healed" in the Eddy faith, and, later, she imagined that her reading a passage or two from *Science and Health* snatched one of her children from the jaws of death. Her *War in Heaven* tells us this story, and it may do no harm to trust it is true.

Mrs. Woodbury has the reputation of never doing things by halves, but of attending to business religiously, and of attending to religion in a business way. Having once entered "Christian Science," she pursued that vocation with great metaphysical and financial success, until suddenly, on the 4th of April, 1896, came the bolt of excommunication.

[44] *War in Heaven: Sixteen Years' Experience in Christian Science, Mind-Healing. By Josephine Curtis Woodbury. Third Edition. Boston, Mass. Press of Samuel Usher, 1897.*

[45] Several suits are pending as this book goes to press. One suit has been "thrown out of court." It should be said, perhaps, that one of Mrs. Woodbury's attorneys, F. W. Peabody, Esq., has such an abhorrence of "Christian Science" in general, that he has been willing to take the part of anybody who could enable him to expose Mrs. Eddy. In this good work may he not be discouraged.

It can readily be understood that conventional respectability is a necessary and profitable department of "The Eddy Church Scientist," and that so shifty an ecclesiastic as "Mother Eddy" can scent opprobrium from afar. Whereto applies certain "Christian-Science" history.

Soon after the excommunication of the apostle Josephine—the latter part of the same year—she was attacked at law by a Mr. Fred D. Chamberlain, in the sum of twenty-five thousand dollars, on the charge that she had alienated the affection and companionship of his wife. The case got into print, and being displayed under large heads in the Boston *Traveler* of December 12th, 1896 and thereafter, a suit was instituted against Mr. Chamberlain and that paper for libel.[46]

It appears from the files of the *Traveler* that its industrious editor collected a large variety of statements, letters, and interviews, for the purpose of showing his readers, that, among Mrs. Woodbury's religious accomplishments—whether it were due to suggestion, elective affinity, hypnotism, or Christian Science—she possessed a mighty gift of drawing simple souls—the rich invariably preferred—into the select congregation of her fleecy followers. Then, at two hundred dollars a follower, she was depicted as converting the sinners of other sects to "Christian Science."

It will be observed that Mrs. Woodbury seemingly dealt in "metaphysics" at cut prices, the "Mother's" regular rate for instruction being three hundred dollars, not two hundred. But, for value received from Mrs. Woodbury's "loyal students"—she, like "the Mother," so naming her disciples—from seven to ten lessons only, according to the *Traveler*, were imparted to them. Then the course was indefinitely repeated, in accordance with the demand that could be created for the healing staples.

Here, to be sure, was something that might have greatly offended "Mother Eddy." Yet daughter Woodbury's cut prices were only colorable, not actual; for, in the frequent repetition of the same wisdom and religiosity to the same "loyal students," she must have done less work for more money than was ever done even in the Mother's college itself.

Again, if we follow newspaper files and court records in the case of the Boston *Traveler*,[47] we are told that Mrs. Woodbury had a family interest in putting on the market certain stock in a hot-air engine—a kind of "Christian Science" stock in which, if her "loyal students" took a religious flyer, their secular dealings would be sure to turn up with the right end in the air. This, perhaps, was a prime investment; but, on investigation, one "loyal student"—plaintiff Chamberlain of the suit we have touched—somehow received the impression, though doubtless through "mortal mind," that the holy engine stock had a slight smell of the Keeley motor. Unetherealized man that he was, this affliction of his base common sense was the

[46] The extraordinary matters of this chapter, however well or ill suppressed, were all published, with great detail, in the issues of the *Traveler* from Dec. 12th to 22d, 1896, and from January 11th to 25th, 1897. Here they have simply been put into brief form, and relieved of all unnecessary harshness. The papers have been preserved for evidence and are in my hands.—G. C.

[47] The story, with many details, in issue of Dec. 14, 1896.

immediate cause, he declared, of all his trouble. His pious wife was unable to bear such an affront to divinity in the person of her "teacher," St. Josephine Woodbury. So the "teacher" stuck to the wife, and the husband was left out in the cold.[48]

That Boston newspaper, the *Traveler*, in spreading the Chamberlain unpleasantness, was assiduously biographical. Particulars can be curtailed. It is only necessary to say that the distinguished Mrs. Woodbury was depicted as a self-made woman who had once been known to plain environments, but who, with preaching, healing, scientific religion and engine-stock, had become financially as well as spiritually beatified. Finally she had reached a shining abode on Commonwealth Avenue—that kind of mansion, in Boston, being the very next thing to "a mansion in the skies."

Her "loyal students," it is true, were not represented by the *Traveler* as having been enriched in the same way. Still, if already wealthy, as most of them were said to be, what was the use of it? Might they not better come unto St. Josephine Woodbury, and cast upon her the dross and sorrow of their material accumulations?

As described in the *Traveler* print, these "loyal students" were, for the most part, rather young people, rich in their own right, or so endeared to their parents that neither gold nor silver, if it could be given, was denied to them. Once in the woods and groves of Teacher Woodbury's "Christian Science" paradise, these charmed innocents were turned into missionaries to their families, where souls might be saved and further possessions might accrue to a blessed instructor. If the heads of these families would not turn from the wicked ways of the world and their own churches, and bring gifts to the shrine of Christian Science, then the "loyal students" were taught to shake the dust from their feet, and depart from among the unholy.

Thus were the Scriptures fulfilled "in Science." But the *Traveler* made it to appear that such doctrine set daughter against father, son against mother, and wife against husband.

So, indeed, the doctrine was made to appear in a letter written by Saint Woodbury herself and published in the *Traveler* over her full name.[49] Therein was this preachment:

"The Bible says that the teachings of Jesus rightly practised, will, *must*, set at variance the members of any household, some of whom do, and some of whom do not, imbibe the faith.... God's will be done. The command is still on the elect to come out from the world, and to separate and to shake the dust from their feet, of any house which will not receive the peace bestowed."

Mrs. Woodbury, having thus justified her religion and her economics by Scripture, proceeded to justify Scripture itself by the Absolute—the example of Mrs. Eddy. St. Josephine went on, in her letter, thus:

"When the Discerner of this Science first apprehended the demands of this Re-

[48] A long story underlies the unfortunate marriage and separation of the lady and gentleman involved in this case. But the facts are not essential to the one and only subject of these pages, "Christian Science."

[49] Issue of Dec. 12, 1896.

ligion and system of ethics, she was forced to withdraw from the Congregational Church.... I have been informed, also, that not one of her family ever held her faith in anything but active contempt."

This latter revelation to St. Woodbury, regarding Saint Mary Baker Eddy and her relatives, is probably true. Others have received the same information. But when the chosen one was rejected of the Baker family, particularly of its affluent members, it is affirmed that the spirit of "Science" arose within Mary, like a mighty tantrum, and, recalling her early likeness to Samuel and the Hebrews, she exclaimed with "immortal mind," "I will yet roll in wealth!" These words of the prophetess-Mother are sweet to the ear of Christian Science, which admonishes its adherents to go and do likewise—assuring them that if steadfast "in Science," they will be sure to stand solid in Dunn and Bradstreet.

It is well that our condition of existence, whatever may be its metaphysical bases, is not all tragedy, but is relieved by a border of comedy. According to a tale of Christian Science, as told by the Boston *Traveler*, Mrs. Woodbury, when in the prime of her healing illumination, with its full returns, felt on one occasion that piety would be advanced if a "loyal student" of hers—a lady of means—should add a promising husband to the true Church. It was done. Then, the ever-watchful "teacher" sent forth on the wedding tour a third "loyal student"—a virgin with her lamp trimmed and burning—to see that neither of the other twain should lapse from grace and the certainty of further contributions.

The complaint against the *Traveler* newspaper got into court on the 11th of January, 1897. Short work was made of it. Notwithstanding all the divine science incarnate in St. Josephine C. Woodbury, His Honor the Judge, Dewey by name, excluded her from the court-room, that she might not contribute to the examination of her witnesses any eye-beams of hypnotism.

As this book is not designed to be improperly personal, but simply an exposition of the claims, doctrines, and effects, of Christian Science, all unnecessary use of individual names must be avoided. But a few are indispensable; and people who are mentioned here have already got themselves corruscatingly into print.

The first witness for Mrs. Woodbury—who turned out also to be the last—was a Mr. Alfred M. Potter. He testified that he was a brother of Mrs. Fred D. Chamberlain—the lady said to be alienated from her husband—and that he and his sister boarded with the Woodburys. He was estranged from his family, he said, except that one sister, but Mrs. Woodbury was not the cause of it.

As the *Traveler* summed up one point of the court-records, Mr. Potter, in the past year, had paid the husband of Mrs. Woodbury thirteen thousand dollars outside of board and room. He had paid Mrs. Woodbury "between a thousand and eleven hundred dollars for instructions for himself." But, in the summer of 1896, there was a European trip for Mr. Potter and the Woodburys. How could a "loyal student," young and wealthy, venture abroad without his "teacher?" And why was not his money well expended for spiritual pleasures, on the way, if St. Josephine and Mr. Woodbury took good care of Mr. Potter, and brought him safe home?

But the most extraordinary matter in connection with Mr. Potter's depositions was a certain quasi-confirmation of a story that came to the *Traveler* and had been published, alleging that, on the authority of Mrs. Woodbury, the ancient and most infinitely closed of all miracles, "the immaculate conception," had been repeated under the advanced dispensation of Mother Eddy's religion. Such was declared by various "loyal students" of Mrs. Woodbury to have been the claim of their exalted "teacher," to whom a son was born, named "Prince," an abbreviation of his full title, "the Prince of Peace." Mr. Potter came short of corroborating the whole of this miracle, but gave substantially the version of it which Mrs. Woodbury presented to the public, after the trial, in the pages of her "War in Heaven." There she says:

"On the morning of June 11th, 1890, there was born to me a baby boy; though, till his sharp birth-cry saluted my ears, I had not realized that prospective maternity was the interpretation of preceding months of physical discomfort.... An hour after the birth I rose. In the afternoon I was up and dressed, and at night dined with my family.... We named our boy Prince Woodbury, partly because he came into our family as a veritable harbinger of peace."

Witness Potter testified that he understood, through Mrs. Woodbury, that "she had no knowledge of the birth of Prince" until she found him with her. This circumstance, he understood, "was through Christian Science."

When Mr. Potter, with a straight, truthful, honest face, gave this testimony, it naturally affected the gravity of the bench, the bar, and all others present, except Christian Scientists. There was reflected from one to another the sardonic smile of "mortal mind." But the case went on until presently a paper was put before Mr. Potter, by counsel for the defense, that it might be identified.

The paper never got before the court. But the contents of it were very peculiar. The paper, in fact, was a brutally blunt form of retraction on the part of Mr. Fred D. Chamberlain, of every derogatory criticism of Mrs. Woodbury he had ever made, and a meek submission to her brand of "Christian Science." In the event of his not signing the paper, he was given to understand that he must depart from the abode of his wife.

The document, it appears, was in the handwriting of the "loyal student," Mrs. Chamberlain, and was dictated by Mrs. Woodbury. But when it was presented to Mr. Chamberlain for his signature, he had not only declined to attach his name to it, but had retained the document.

The Woodbury counsel quickly protested against the admission of such evidence, and the protest was judicious; for was not the whole case of "alienation" substantially set down on that paper? Hence, too, what would become of the libel-suit? But the court decided that the evidence was admissible. Then, in such a shocking plight, what could an able Woodbury lawyer do but decline, with virtuous indignation, to go on further with the case? The short of it was that Judge Dewey discharged the defendants, reprimanded the prosecution, and the noisy *Traveler* had everything its own way.[50]

---

[50] There were really two papers handed to Mr. Chamberlain, and he was to take his choice between them. The case, too, was withdrawn, not wholly on account of one thing,

As for the Chamberlain suit for damages "in Science," it was not pursued to the monetary end. It was soon ascertained that the wife really had more affection for her delectable "teacher" than any "loyal student" could be expected to have for a mere husband. As a business necessity, a divorce was then procured by Mr. Chamberlain, on the ground of desertion, and the twain went separate ways.

It was not proved in Mrs. Woodbury's libel suit against the *Traveler* that St. Josephine had claimed the full import of the *Traveler's* story about her "Prince." The proceedings, we have seen, were prematurely stopped. But, after the newspaper's legal victory, it published sworn statements from a number of people who would have been its witnesses had the trial gone on. The most important was one made by Hon. George E. Macomber, an ex-mayor of Augusta, Maine.[51] In the regular form of a legal deposition he declared that he had known Mrs. Woodbury for several years, his acquaintance with her having come through his wife, who had taken lessons of her. He said:

"My wife came one day and said Mrs. Woodbury had had a child down at Ocean Point which was a 'Second Christ,' was immaculately conceived, and that it was the duty of her students to make presents to this 'Second Christ.'"

Mr. Macomber declined to make presents, and, according to his statement, his wife's "eyes were opened," after a while, and she "pulled out" of "Science."

The *Traveler's* other witnesses may pass. It is only essential to say that they were numerous, and that they all agreed with Mr. Macomber. One of them testified, in an interview, that he had once gone so far in neglect of his own family as to make a will in favor of "the Prince of Peace." But our direct point here is only this. — There would seem to be no doubt that St. Josephine Woodbury's "loyal students," far and wide, were called upon to bear gifts to her celestial son. Hence, his origin had palpable use as a financial mystery, whatever may have been its precise theological bearings.

In "Christian Science," the doctrine here recorded has been logically coupled with another doctrine — that of inconnubiality in wedlock. This tenet, we can see, like the former, might result in money, goods and bequests, for some attractive "teacher," which might otherwise be squandered by a "student" in raising a family.

But the principle here imbedded "in Science" has not been special to Mrs. Woodbury. Mother Eddy herself is the crystal background of all good things, and this one, with the rest, must be credited to the fountain of universal originality, *Science and Health*.[52] The pure simplicity of any being who can seriously read that book to the end, inevitably fits him to maintain with Christian Scientists, that, if children be not given to parents under physical laws, the science of perfect purity will ultimately evolve *"Children of the Soul." "My husband and I,"* recently but many things which Mrs. Woodbury's lawyer found it impossible to contend against. But the most direct cause of the withdrawal is the one given.

[51] Boston *Traveler*, January 21, 1897.

[52] Until it is learned that generation rests on no sexual basis, let marriage continue. Spirit will ultimately claim its own, and the voices of physical sense be forever hushed. — *Science and Health*, page 274.

exclaimed a vestal matron of Mrs. Eddy's following, "have long lived together as brother and sister: isn't it beautiful?" "Perhaps it is," replied another matron, thus addressed, "but I am told it is generally impracticable, except in Boston."

When last heard from, our contemporary "Prince of Peace" was a pretty school-boy of wit beyond his years. May the world smile kindly on "Prince Woodbury," who is in nowise to blame for any new-fangled religion; but may heaven preserve him from any further involution with the sacraments of "Christian Science."

Before bidding adieu to the heroine-martyr of our present chapter, one more instance must be given of her work in a careless world—a very sad instance, not to be treated lightly.

Among Mrs. Josephine Woodbury's "loyal students" for some time preceding the year 1897, was a hand-maiden of "Christian Science," one Mary Nash. The story of poor little Mary was told in the Boston *Traveler*,[53] chiefly in the words of her father, when that paper was sued for libel "in Science."

Mary Nash, as we summarize that story, lived at Augusta, Maine, and her father, like our witness Macomber, had been a mayor of that city. He was a busy man, but one who loved his daughter, and kept her in funds for what he regarded as harmless fads and amusements.

Mary joined the "loyal students." Then, little by little, she absented herself from Augusta, making frequent pilgrimages to Boston. The pilgrimages grew in duration, until her home was seldom her habitation. "Teacher" Woodbury had not only changed her heart, but her whole tenor of mortal life, and Mary was completely born again into the most progressed fears and phases of "Christian Science."

Letters followed to her father, asking for money, and demanding that he and all his house should join "the loyal students." He forwarded the money as occasion required, but his unregenerate neck stiffly declined "Science." So Mary went no more to her father for weeks and months together. He sent her mother and brother to her, with prayers that she return to the family hearth-stone, if not to the family church. But she was always sequestered from the influence of her relatives, by some "loyal student" or other in the Woodbury collection of dutiful freaks.

Mary's soul was much disturbed at times, notwithstanding the religio-scientific consolations of her surrounding guardians. She began to demonstrate, in her own scattered little person, the one everlasting assumption of "Christian Science," that the human body is an illusion to be dispelled. In other words, Mary Nash was fast sinking into what ordinary doctors of medicine and divinity term illness, and it became extreme.

Then, not for the first time, her father, went to Boston himself, to take, if possible, his daughter back to his care and her mother's heart, at the Augusta home. But still, still—unless by some accident of a moment—she was always under the eye and the power of a "metaphysical" keeper. Then Mary said "no"—she "could not leave the fount of Christian Science." So she stayed in Boston; for she was of

---

[53] January 15, 1897.

age, and could select her castle and companionship while she had the ways and means to maintain them.

Now what could a poor law-abiding citizen of New England, who had once been a mayor, do in such a case? Had Mary's father been a wild citizen of the West or the South, he might have taken his handy "gun" along with him, and removed his child or "cleaned out the ranch." But Maine and Massachusetts are too subdued for such stringent remedies. So Mayor Nash mourned of "hypnotism," and offered—the distracted father that he was—five hundred dollars, to release his daughter from the blessings of her religion. This mercenary offer was spurned, as suspect perchance in legal and ecclesiastic form; but the way was pointed out in which the money might be received for lessons in Christian Science, at the Woodbury cut-rates.

Meanwhile, it being ascertained that Mary Nash had a modest bank-account in her name, the money was sent for, by herself nominally, but visibly through a person in the number seven shoes of a "loyal student." The bank men—who were not "in Science"—declined to pay Mary's demand, and referred the matter to her father. He agreed with the bank in holding the proceeds of his daughter's account, and his very stomach, not to say his soul, rejected the thought of exchanging cash for religious instruction from Mrs. Josephine C. Woodbury.

So little Mary Nash became of no further promise to "Christian Science." And there was no time to lose. Mary was plainly departing from the state of deception—certainly such to *her*—called "earthly life." Hastily, at last, she was permitted to journey home with her father, and presently the sad man laid his daughter away in what to him was death.[54]

From the history of "Christian Science"—set down in these pages as the thing really is—it must be clear to anybody not quite emptied of all "mortal sense" that Mrs. Josephine C. Woodbury has been the most logical sequence, the most practical outcome, of the whole firmamental illumination.

But, that the Church of St. Bunco should grow and prosper—or should even hold its own among its honest innocents—it has been necessary for Mrs. Eddy not only to preach "love" and "purity" in general, but to draw the line of practical conduct somewhere short of blackmail, larceny and homicide. St. Josephine Woodbury never committed a sin in her life. Sin has no reality "in Science." Her "loyal students" would all have testified that she was equal to any of the angels, if not better than the highest. Yet a hard world around her, not understanding "true religion," began to fancy, say in 1896, that she was not, every second, fulfilling

---

[54] I have seen what I suppose to be true copies of a series of letters written by Mary Nash and different members of her family, with one or two from some of Mrs. Woodbury's "loyal students." The letters might possibly be taken to show that inharmony existed in the Nash family, and that the daughter stayed away from father, mother and brothers on that account, instead of being, if such was the case, just where a sensible and affectionate daughter was most needed. The letters, at any rate, show the most united affection for *her*, and more than willingness to do anything she asked, if she would only return to her home. When finally she did so, two physicians, according to Mr. Nash, declared her to be under hypnotic control. Letters, under hypnotism, are suspect.—G. C.

all the ten commandments. Then, besides her *War in Heaven*, the lady has written another book, called *Christian Voices*, in which, the thought having been long imputed to her, she asked the question, "Who shall succeed Mrs. Eddy?" As *Science and Health* declares there is no death, and as "Mother Eddy" is specially immortal, St. Josephine's carnal talk of the "Christian Science succession" was naturally regarded "in Science" as worse than blasphemy. Thus many things worked together against St. Josephine Woodbury, until at last she sat on "Mother" Eddy's burning fagots and wore the crown of martyrdom.

Thereat the world did not come to an end, but went right on with the production of quacks, dupes, and "loyal students."

CHAPTER XI.

METAPHYSICS.[55]

"Mother Eddy" and her flock "in Science" derive a considerable part of their income from a glib use of the word "Metaphysics." But what the "Church Scientist" has omitted to learn about the real import of that word would make a volume even larger than *Science and Health*.

As unreservedly admitted in our present essay, there is no trouble about a spiritual derivation of the universe. In the declaratory, religious form, the New Testament is a sufficient example of this doctrine. In the philosophical form the names of Plato and Aristotle, both of whom resolved all things into the principle of "Mind," summarized the subject for the ancient world. The modern world has now given three hundred years to the same theme, and, however well or ill aware of the fact, has reached the same end, but wholly without the assistance of any pushing, dodging adventuress, with a little set of abstract ideas and much screaming of "Science."

Leaving lighter themes for the moment, let us venture on a brief survey of this ground.

There are just two possible ways of analyzing things. One way is to set the world with its particulars before the eye, look at it, and accept what we see. Then we may go to work on phenomena, dissecting and generalizing. This is the way of physics—a road that *never* leads to *meta*-physics. It is the common turnpike of material science—of "positivism." In it travel all such men, say, as Dr. Ernst Hæckel: also all such men as the late Parson John Jasper, the colored preacher of Virginia, who, seeing the sun move round the earth, settled the fact in that way.

The one other way of dissecting the universe is to examine the *means* through which things are presented to us, and thus to ascertain what effect the means may have in the production and nature of the things. This method of investigation has ultimated in what has been summed up as "Scientific Idealism."

Scientific idealism is the knowledge which every one may get even from his first lessons in optics, that things of matter—the objects of our five senses—are constituted such through the structure and action of these senses themselves. That

---

[55] The chapters of our book from XI. to XVI. inclusive, were, in substance, written at the request of Dr. William T. Harris, United States Commissioner of Education, and published in his *Journal of Speculative Philosophy* for December, 1893, under the caption of "The Secret of Kant." These chapters, while too abstruse for light readers, really explain what "Christian Science" ignorantly chatters about as "Metaphysics."—G. C.

is to say, material things—whatever we see or feel, hear, taste or smell—while existent and real—while practically what every one takes them to be—are *made so* through *relativity*. Or, as Kant put it, every "phenomenon"—meaning every object or fact of sensation—is a "*re*-presentation"; that is, some lot of effects on our sensuous nature, bound together into a unity of them, the unity thus formed becoming an object of awareness, a "percept."

Scientific idealism does not question the given duality of the cosmos, which appears to us as what we call "mind and matter." Here are *we*; out there, indubitably apart from us, are other things, involving another source. But scientific idealism has found that this source is itself quite other than the things we connect with it, and can properly be described in this connection only as *source of impact*. It has nothing to do with matter, in the common acceptation. It enters *into* matter, being the ultimate non-ego, the objective background, of every phenomenon. But, in all material things, this background is *transformed* by contact with subjective sense (in us or other organisms), and "matter" is really the fusion, the compound, the third term, of these two elemental principles.

This momentous truth, though mystically reached in the old tenet of India that "matter is illusion," and though touched understandingly by Carneades in Greece, was first clearly seen, in the manner of modern science, by the remarkably solid Englishman, Thomas Hobbes.

"Qualities called sensible" [said Hobbes] "are, in the object that causeth them, but so many several motions of the matter by which it presseth our organs diversely.... Because the image in vision, consisting of color and shape, is the knowledge we have of the qualities of the object of that sense, it is no hard matter for a man to fall into this opinion, that the same color and shape are the very qualities themselves."

But, concluded Hobbes:

"The subject wherein color and image are inherent is not the object or thing seen.... There is nothing without us (really) which we call an image or color.... The said image or color is but an apparition unto us of *the motion, agitation, or alteration, which the object worketh in the brain, or spirits, or some internal substance of the head....* As in vision, so also in conceptions that arise from the other senses, the subject of their inference is not the object, but the sentient."

When John Locke began his great "Essay" on *The Human Understanding*, and posited mind in its first estate as a passive nonentity—a "blank tablet"—he had no vital conception of scientific idealism. But, in the patient thinking of twenty years, such a man could not fail to come upon the law, though he saw it only in part, and did not work it out. This work was carried a great way beyond him, by the acute and learned Bishop Berkeley, who showed from practical science, especially through his investigation of "vision," that nothing in the universe has any actual being, apart from a universal element, that, wherever it may be posited, can alone be called Mind.

Since Berkeley, no philosophical thinker, perhaps, of any significance, anywhere in the world, has questioned the "ideality" of "material things." Even Reid, as the philosopher of "common sense," declared that

> "No man can conceive any sensation to resemble any known quality of bodies. Nor can any man show, by any good argument, that all our sensations might not have been as they are, though no body, nor quality of body, had ever existed."

Hume's comprehension of Scientific idealism was complete to his day, and was completely stated. He said:

"'Tis not our body we perceive when we regard our limbs and members, but certain impressions which enter by the senses; so that the ascribing a real and corporeal existence to these impressions, or to their objects, is an act of the mind difficult to explain."

The idealism of recent "materialistic" philosophers, such as Herbert Spencer and the school of "Positivists," has been most carefully expressed by John Stuart Mill, in his statement that "Matter is a Permanent Possibility of Sensation."

"If" [said Mr. Mill] "I am asked whether I believe in matter, I ask whether the questioner accepts this definition of it. If he does, I believe in matter; and so do all Berkeleians. In any other sense than this I do not."

For an easy, popular view of the principle of scientific idealism, perhaps nothing has been better said than by Thomas Carlyle, in his review of Novalis.

"To a transcendentalist [says Carlyle] matter has an existence, but only as a phenomenon. Were *we* not there, neither would *it* be there: it is a mere relation, or rather the result of a relation between our living souls and the great First Cause; and depends for its apparent qualities on our bodily and mental organs; having itself no intrinsic qualities; being, in the common sense of the word, nothing. The tree is green and hard, not of its own natural virtue, but simply because my eye and my hand are fashioned so as to discern such and such appearances under such and such conditions. Nay, as an idealist might say, even on the most popular grounds, *must* it not be so? Bring a sentient being with eyes a little different, fingers ten times harder than mine, and to him that thing which I call tree shall be yellow and soft, as truly as to me it is green and hard. Form the nervous structure in all points the reverse of mine, and this same tree shall not be combustible and heat-producing, but dissoluble and cold-producing; not high and convex, but deep and concave; shall simply have *all* properties exactly the reverse of those attributed to it. There is no tree there; but only a manifestation of power from something which is not *I*. The same is true of material nature at large, of the whole visible universe, with all its movements, figures, accidents and qualities."

Scientific idealism, as far as we have gone with it, has now become one of the *"exact"* sciences—as much so as physics. It has been simply the result of continuous and innumerable experiments in natural philosophy, for three centuries. There is no need of going into these physical particulars, after they have been put into the school-books of children and explained in popular lectures. One more quotation must suffice. Mr. G. H. Lewes, in his *Biographical History of Philosophy*, tells us that

"The radical error of those who believe that we perceive things *as they are*, consists in mistaking a metaphor for a fact, and believing that the mind is a mirror in which external objects are reflected. But, as Bacon finely says, 'The human understanding is like an *unequal mirror* to the rays of things, which, *mixing its own nature with the nature of things, distorts and perverts them.*' We attribute heat to fire, and color to the flower, heat and color being states of our consciousness, occasioned by the fire and the flower under certain conditions. Perception is nothing more than a *state of the percipient*, a state of consciousness.... Of every change in our sensation we are conscious, and in time we learn to give definite names and forms to the causes of these changes. But in the fact of consciousness there is nothing *beyond* consciousness. In our perceptions we are conscious only of the changes which have taken place within us.... All we can do is to identify certain *external appearances* with certain internal changes.... We conclude, therefore, that the world *per se* in nowise resembles the world as it appears to us. Perception is an Effect; and its truth is not the truth of *resemblance*, but of *relation*.... Light, color, sound, taste, are all states of Consciousness; what they are beyond consciousness ... we cannot know, we cannot imagine, because we can only conceive them *as* we know them. Light, with its myriad forms and colors—Sound, with its thousand-fold life—make Nature what Nature appears to us. But they do not exist, *as such*, apart from our consciousness; they are investitures with which we clothe the world. Nature, in her insentient solitude is an eternal Darkness—an eternal Silence."

CHAPTER XII.

FURTHER ANALYSIS OF THE UNIVERSE.

In a previous chapter, some special reference has been made to a little German professor named Immanuel Kant. He was born at Königsberg, in 1724. In 1781 he wrote a book which he called "The Critique of Pure Reason." This provokingly modest title, as already said, covered, in reality, *the analysis of mind and matter, time and space*. It was the most far-reaching piece of purely intellectual work that had ever been given to the world. It has split the heads of hundreds of "philosophers." Certain thinkers have fancied they have thought beyond it, and have supposed it to be laid on the shelf of "deceased philosophy." Meanwhile, we are told, the universities "are returning to the study of Kant." Better still, some of them are even beginning to understand him. Here we shall take him straight, paying no attention to any of the side issues in which he was apt to cover himself up.[56]

Kant, so learned that he was said to "know everything," was completely acquainted with the whole trend of British philosophy, from John Locke to David Hume. He was saturated, too, with the physical sciences. So his first real step in his *Critique of Pure Reason* was to found himself on the all-inclusive law of scientific idealism. Immanuel Kant did not fool with this law. He did not test it, prove it, and then let it slip out of a loose, greasy mind, as an airy nothing of no practical consequence. He grasped it, and held it, as the bed-rock of all thought and all things. It is a pity he omitted to say so at the very first touch of his work. But he said it clearly enough when he happened to get ready. Thus, for instance:[57]

"In order to prevent any misunderstanding, it will be requisite, in the first place, to recapitulate, as clearly as possible, what our opinion is with respect to *the fundamental nature of our sensuous cognition in general*. We have intended, then, to say that all our intuition is nothing but the re-presentation of phenomena; that the things which we intuite are not in themselves the same as our re-presentations of them in intuition, nor are their relations so constituted as they appear to us; and that *if we take away the subject, or even only the subjective constitution of our senses in general*, then *not only the nature and relations of objects* in space and time, *but even space and time themselves disappear*.... What may be the nature of objects considered as things in themselves, and without reference to the receptivity of our sensibility,

---

[56] As this book, including the present chapter, is for readers who may or may not understand German, our quotations from Kant are taken from his *Critique* as in the old familiar, accessible translation by J. M. D. Meiklejohn (Bohn's Philosophical Library—edition of 1860).

[57] *Critique of Pure Reason*; General Remarks on Transcendental Æsthetic, p. 35.

is quite unknown to us."

Again, in closing his dissection of space, Kant said:

"Objects are quite unknown to us in themselves, and *what we call outward objects* are nothing else but mere *re-presentations of our sensibility*, whose form is space, but whose real correlate, the thing in itself, is not known by means of these representations, nor ever can be, but respecting which, in experience, no inquiry is ever made."

Once more:

"The faculty of sensibility not only does not present us with any indistinct and confused cognition of objects as things in themselves, but, in fact, gives us *no knowledge of these* at all. On the contrary, as soon as we abstract in thought *our own subjective nature*, the object re-presented, with the properties ascribed to it by sensuous intuition, *entirely disappears, because it was only this subjective nature that determined the form of the object as a phenomenon.*"

After awhile, under the maddening caption of "The Possibility of a Conjunction of the Manifold Representations given by Sense,"[58] our German professor virtually crowded his whole work into this one paragraph:

"The manifold content in our re-presentations can be given in an intuition which is merely sensuous—in other words, is nothing but susceptibility; and the form of this intuition can exist *a priori* in our faculty of representation, without being anything else but the mode in which the subject is affected. But the conjunction (*conjunctio*) of a manifold in intuition never can be given by the senses; it cannot therefore be contained in the pure form of sensuous intuition, for it is a spontaneous act of the faculty of re-presentation. And as we must, to distinguish it from sensibility, entitle this faculty *understanding*, so all conjunction, whether conscious or unconscious, be it of the manifold in intuition, sensuous or non-sensuous, or of several conceptions, is an act of the understanding. To this act we shall give the general appellation of *synthesis*, thereby to indicate, at the same time, that *we cannot represent anything as conjoined in the object without having previously conjoined it ourselves.*"

As to comprehend this paragraph is to analyze the universe, let us grapple with it.

Impatient Dr. Sam. Johnson once kicked a stone to refute Berkeley. Let us take that stone, as a clump of matter, and treat it with the head instead of the foot.

"The manifold content in our re-presentations," says Kant, "can be given in an intuition which is merely sensuous." This means simply that the various properties of the "re-presentation" or "intuition" called a stone are "effects on the senses." The color, the texture, the weight, the size—every one of all such "material" attributes—exist, as they are, solely by relation to *me*, or to some other being in whom is organized the element of "sense." Matter is *made* of impact—impact between its objective background ("the noumenon" or "noumena") and some sort or degree of subjectivity. Without these two terms, their product of interaction, their

---

[58] *Critique*; Transcendental Logic, p. 80.

third term, matter, is *not*. So "the manifold content" of a "re-presentation"—or, what is the same thing, the properties of a material object—are "nothing but susceptibility."

By "the form of intuition," Kant meant, as he has repeatedly explained, the *plural quality* of space and time. Space is made of *spaces*; time of *times*; and the plural contents (always such) of matter can only exist under the plural contents of space and time—that is, in sections of space and sequences of time, these sections and sequences being the intrinsic character, the divisible quality, the essential "form" of space and time as total units or completed things. And the nature of space and time need not be anything more *objective* than the nature of matter in general, but can be derived, too, from "the mode in which the subject is affected." "But," says Kant, "*all conjunction*" is "an act of the understanding," and "can not be contained in the pure form of sensuous intuition"; by which he means that time could never be a conjunct of times, space a conjunct of spaces, nor a stone the conjunct of its properties—each a "synthesis" of a "manifold content"—unless made so by the synthetical unity of *a priori* mind.

Kant attributes *"unconscious"* action to the *"understanding"*—the unconscious action of "conjunction" or "synthesis." His phrase has been a perpetual stumbling-block to his readers, but he meant exactly what he said. Unconscious mental synthesis is what he afterward designated as "the synthesis of *apprehension*."

"By the term *synthesis* of apprehension [said he], I understand the combination of the manifold in an empirical intuition, whereby perception, that is, empirical consciousness of the intuition (as phenomenon), is possible."

Kant talks of "making the empirical intuition of a house into a perception, by apprehension of the manifold contained therein," and says that "the *necessary unity of space* and of my *external sensuous intuition* lies at the foundation of this act." The "manifold" contained in an "empirical intuition"—take the stone we have used for an example—is simply the diversity of "properties," constituting the object—the color, texture, size, weight, and the rest of them; and these properties are "effects of sense." Every one of them is a relation to subjectivity, a result of impact *on* subjectivity, and is in the *object* only as reflecting or *re*-presenting there the sensuous nature of a *subject*. But these various "effects on various senses," these merely subjective separates—how do they *get united* into *one thing*? What constitutes the unity of sensuous manifolds? Every phenomenon being an essential plurality—a lot of "sense-effects"—what closes together the various effects on various human senses, called the properties of a stone, into the one phenomenal object, the stone itself. To this end there must be some common subjective ground of those subjective things, "effects on sense." There must be some subjective unity in which those subjective pluralities all merge, for only as *merged* do they get to be an *object*. Now, a common subjective ground of various effects on various senses can only be a common *awareness of them*—a *synthetical unity of apprehension*, or just instinctive, automatic consciousness in the germ. This must be common to all the senses together, and to each sense separately. What, for example, is seeing, but the simple awareness of sight? What is touch, but the simple awareness of feeling? What is any "intuition," which means any taking-in of any phenomenon, but a common awareness, however rudimental or developed, of some conjoined diversity of effects on sense?

It must be added here, as vital to the full comprehension of the genesis of matter, that not only every material object, like our example, the stone, is made of essential plurality of sense-effects, but that *every separate property* of an object is also made of like plurality. No object, and no property of an object, is, or can be, single, unal, or, in other words, *anything*, until constructed so, in sense, by the "unconscious understanding" thereof—the synthetical unity of instinctive, automatic "apprehension." To realize this fact, it is only necessary to remember that every property of anything, say the hardness of a stone, is a compound relation between the impact of some ultimate non-ego on the sense of touch, and the peculiar nature of the sense itself: so the property of hardness must contain *essential diversity*, something from each of *two fundamental sources*. As Aristotle, from his ontological investigations, found that matter, if regarded as an absolute independence—an unrelated thing in itself—is *no thing*, but only chaotic indeterminateness—formless "potentiality"—so Kant, from his psychological inquiry—his dissection of phenomena as existent through perception—found the same truth in deeper significance. The *entire principle of unity*, Whether in a feeling, a thought, a material object, or the universe as a whole, *can only exist through the principle of mind*.

Here is the very bottom of the discoveries of Kant, and the basis, also, of all things.

. Mind, then, in its lowest state, is what Kant, "to distinguish it from sensibility," entitled "unconscious understanding." There used to be an old saw in philosophy—still, indeed, at work—to the effect that "there is nothing in the mind that was not first in sense." Leibnitz, adding a piece to the saw, said: "Except mind itself." Leibnitz affirmed, that is, that sense always *contains* mind—that mind is *in* sense as a component of it, and that without mind there is no sense at all. What Leibnitz perceived and asserted, Kant *proved* by "observation and induction"—by analyzing phenomena under the law of scientific idealism. Mind in sense—the mind of sense—is just *automatic animal awareness*, just "simple apprehension," undeveloped, and in the lowest animal life not to be developed, into "apperception," the *conscious* stage of understanding, capable of forming a *concept*.

Well, in the genesis of a stone, or any other material object, certain effects on sense are merged in the unit they compose, by reception into the "synthetical unity of apprehension." The stone is *created* in this way. Its own objective unity—its wholeness, or "*form*" as a stone—is thus the derivation, the manufactured product, of *subjectivity as a cosmic element*, an element "*a priori*" to the existence of any possible phenomenon.

The stone, however, *is* unmistakably objective—is just the palpable thing that everybody takes it to be, out there in space. This is a given *fact of perception*—something, as Kant said, "never questioned in experience." As such *fact*, how can it be accounted for, when we know, at the same time, that the stone is nothing but a plexus of subjective states? How does the bunch of *internal impressions* get *externalized*? What is the cause of this reflex, this "*re-presentation*"? It must be something inherent in the principle of *apprehension itself,* or the plexus of impressions would necessarily stay within us. Being wrought internally, it would remain internal. Hence, this "apprehension"—this element of instinctive synthetical awareness— must be in its nature a *double*—an entity which reproduces, or throws out before itself, whatever lot of sense-effects it receptively synthesizes, or binds together in a sheaf, known as some object. But all this, summed up, means only that mind, even in its lowest form of "unconscious understanding"—the simple automatic apprehension which shuts together certain effects on sense into a totality of them—must, *as being apprehension,* necessarily, though instinctively, apprehended its own product. Here is the full explanation of the amusing, iron-clad conception of Hobbes, that an "image," or a "color," is but an apparition unto us of "motion, agitation, or alteration" in some "internal substance of the head."

The self-reflexiveness of "apprehension" is precisely the same thing, *in germ,* that the self-reflexiveness of "apperception" is, in *full self-consciousness.*

The self-reflexiveness of apprehension, in the manufacture of phenomena, was named by Kant *"the transcendental synthesis of imagination"*—the word "imagination" standing on its roots, and meaning *the image-making faculty.* Phenomena, as reflex-conjuncts of sense-effects, are "produced"—put out—by this second function of apprehension; so Kant said he sometimes called it "productive imagination." It is that function of pure elemental, or *a priori* awareness, which "*re*-presents" itself in the constitution of every object, as its *unity,* but a unity *shaped* according to some object's filling of senses-effects. Hence Kant says:

"This synthesis of the manifold of sensuous intuition, which is possible and necessary *a priori,* may be called figurative synthesis (*synthesis speciosa*)."

Thus Kant found mind in sense, "unconscious understanding," the instinctive awareness of animal susceptibility, as it existed in himself, to be the literal objective basis of all phenomena—the first "material" unity of every "material thing." And he found this elemental source of all unity to be an innate self-activity—a self-seeing mirror, as it were—a double of receptiveness and reflectiveness. Here, at last, was the actual, *living thing,* of which Locke's "blank-tablet" had long been the still-born, stone figure.

Mr. Herbert Spencer, in his remarkable investigation of "The Principles of Psychology," posits "mind" as always implied in sentiency, and as necessary to the genesis of any phenomenon, even the "first nervous shock" of a sensitive being. Recognizing the law of scientific idealism, he has seen, too, that our objective world is made up, at the perceptional outset, of such shocks. Again, he has proved, with great detail, that the action of mind is always of one general nature, whether in the lowest animal instinct or the highest conscious reason. But back at the first nervous shock, Mr. Spencer *stops* with mind, and says that at the next regress it becomes "unknowable." Yet nearly a hundred years before this investigation Kant showed precisely what this so-called "unknowable" *is.* He showed that mind, in all stages and states—mind in itself—is a synthetical unity of awareness. In germ, as "unconscious understanding"—as the mind of sense—its function is to be simply apprehensive of, and thus to conjoin in its instinctive cognizance, some "manifold" contained in a "nervous shock," or in various sense-effects, into some *unity*; which then, as *itself apprehended*, or *made a reflex*, becomes an impression, an image, an object.

CHAPTER XIII.

A SPECIAL LOOK AT SPACE AND TIME.

Through scientific idealism, fully examined, Kant proved that matter is a manufacture of sense. We have not followed the order of his work, but have gone straight to the heart of it. His own beginning was the dissection of space and time. Still, he implied therein, if only in one remark, all that has here been stated.

"If I take [says Kant] from our representation of a body, all that the understanding thinks as belonging to it, as substance, force, divisibility, and also whatever belongs to sensation, as impenetrability, hardness, color, there is still something left us from this empirical intuition, namely *extension and shape*. These belong to pure intuition, which exists *a priori* in the mind, as a mere form of sensibility, and without any real object of the senses or any sensation."

Students of Kant have known, in a general way, that he attributed "extension" to "bodies," as derived by them from *a priori* mind. *Space* is so derived; hence all things *in* space, which is the "form," the "condition" of their existence, must partake of its nature, which is pure extension, pure "given quantity," as he designates it. But why does the *shape* of a material body belong to "pure intuition," and *come from mind*? Simply because the shape (let it be of a stone) is merely the *objected "synthesis of apprehension,"* in which the properties of the stone, as impressions of sense, are *unified*, but in accordance with their special variety. The shape is their "figurative synthesis," their *"synthesis speciosa."* Now, in the meaning of Kant, and in the nature of the case, space is *made* in precisely the same *manner* as a stone; only the stone is full of diverse properties—special effects on sense, got from some impinging background of matter—some "noumenon"—while space has no properties at all, except additions and divisions of *itself*—spaces. In other words, the stone is a *special* relation between mental synthesis and sensuous susceptibility, the latter being in particular impact with some noumenal non-ego, and being definitely *filled* from it. Space, on the other hand, is a *general* relation between the same mental synthesis and the same sensuous susceptibility, the latter holding *no contents* from any noumenon, yet being recipient to *all* possibility of noumenal impact. Hence, space is just "the synthesis of apprehension" itself, set in self-reflex, objected, phenomenated. The stone, in its unity, its form, its "shape," is this objected synthesis of apprehension, *filled* with certain sensuous effects. The synthesis of apprehension, again, as the condition of any special "shape" into which it may be stuffed, is of course *a priori* to *the* stuffed shape; so space is *a priori* to the stone in space. Once again, space is the outward representation, the very double to the eye, of the synthesis of apprehension; for space is just the *visible synthesis of the apprehended*—the transparent base of co-existence for all external things.

It must be remembered that the synthesis of apprehension, as the "mind" of "sense," is itself a *double*, containing the pure conjunctive unity of "unconscious understanding" as an active factor, and susceptibility to impact as a passive factor. In the conjoined relation of these two factors every material phenomenon gets to exist; so there must be *some* relation of space to *every* external object, and to *all* external objects—which is to say at once that space is *infinite*, both in extent and divisibility, so far as it can apply to objects *at all*.

And here, too, is the reason that the contained character, the constituent quality, of space—meaning what Kant termed the "form of the intuition"—is essentially plural. This constituent quality of space is a *re*-presentation of mind, as at once active and passive, receptive and reflexive—as fundamental *a priori* self-separateness. But *space itself*, as a *whole*, is the *synthesis* of this self-separateness. It is self-unity of self-separateness, *materialized*. Space, made of spaces, is a thing identical in form and contents. Kant said:

"Space *re*-presented as an *object* (as geometry really requires it to be) contains more than the mere *form of the intuition*; namely, a combination of the manifold given according to the form of sensibility into a representation that can be intuited; so the *form of the intuition* gives us merely the manifold, but the *formal intuition* gives unity of re-presentation. In the 'Æsthetic,' [the first division of *The Critique of Pure Reason*], I regarded this unity as belonging entirely to sensibility, for the purpose of indicating that it antecedes all conceptions, although it presupposes a synthesis which does not belong to sense, through which, however, all our conceptions of space and time are possible.... By means of this unity alone (the understanding determining the sensibility) space and time are given as intuitions."

It is easy enough to follow out the genesis of time, in the same way as the genesis of space. The constituent quality of space and time is the same in both, and is subject in both to the same act of synthesis, in order that the essential plurality of "the form of intuition" may be created into the unity of "the formal intuition" itself—the single thing, space or time. But time is the "form" of "*in*-ternal sense," as Kant put it, while space is the "form" of "*ex*-ternal sense"—sense being to Kant not its physical organs (which are matter), but mental *susceptibility* as distinguished from mental *synthesis*. Every phenomenon in space is made of active subjective-synthesis, passive subjective-susceptibility, and noumenal impact. Space and time themselves are made of the synthesis and the susceptibility alone. But pure synthesis, which means just pure identity of awareness, can *have* no "susceptibility," cannot be *occupied*, without *change of state*; and any change of state in a pure general awareness forms succession of states, or, as Kant said, "*generates time*." But conjunction, again, of synthesis and susceptibility must be the relating of separates, with reference to the objective as well as the subjective factor. As objective effect this relation is pure co-existence of separates in time, through outness from each other—space. All objects, impressions, "effects of sense," must take the order of time; but "objects of internal sense" (feelings, or emotions), having no direct filling from noumena, are not objects in space. Thus, while space is pure synthesis of apprehension *ex*-ternally objected, time is the same pure synthesis of apprehension *in*-ternally objected.

CHAPTER XIV.

CREATIVE MIND FURTHER PROBED.

The inmost secret of the universe lies in Kant's four words, "the synthesis of apprehension," or what he more elaborately termed "the transcendental synthesis of the image-making faculty."

"It is an operation [he says] of the understanding on sensibility, and the *first* application of the understanding to objects of possible intuition, and at the same time *the basis for the exercise of the other functions of that faculty*."

It has been intently presented to view in these pages, because it focalises and explains the whole law of scientific idealism, and is the one most important as well as abstruse fact in the genesis of things.

But having duly dealt with this point, it must now be said that "the synthesis of apprehension," *alone* and *ungrown*, is altogether inadequate to give form to an object, in the full import of that word. For an *object* is something held distinct by itself, in connection with another object, or with various objects. "*Unconscious* understanding" cannot form such connection and distinction, but can only blindly manufacture single intuitions, affording at most what Kant termed "a rhapsody of perceptions," in which no one would be first or last, or anything at all when past. A fish-worm, perhaps, has such a "rhapsody of perceptions" for its objective world. In the world of man the *a priori* element of intelligence which shapes it must be objected in the phase of consciousness proper, or "apperception," as well as "simple apprehension."

In noting the difference between the synthesis of apprehension and the synthesis of apperception, Kant said:

"It is one and the same spontaneity which, at one time under the name of imagination, at another under that of understanding, produces conjunction in the manifold of intuition."

"Apperception" is simply apprehension *apprehended*, or mind adequate to self-conception and so to conceptions in general. That there can be a stone, as known to a *human being*, there must be a synthesis of sense-effects (its properties), in which they are distinguished among themselves, and of which objects as wholes are distinguished from each other. A synthesis of this kind presupposes not merely "unconscious understanding," but understanding that recognizes *itself* in connecting all things else.

"I am conscious [said Kant] of my identical self in relation to all the variety of representations given to me in intuition, because I call all of them *my* representations.... The thought, 'These representations, given in intuition, belong all of them to me,' is just the same as 'I unite them in one self-conscious.'... Synthetical unity of the manifold in intuition, as given *a priori*, is therefore the foundation of the identity of apperception itself, which antecedes *a priori* all determinate thought. But the conjunction of representations into a conception is not to be found in objects themselves ... but is on the contrary, an operation of the understanding itself, which is nothing more than the faculty of conjoining *a priori*, and of bringing the variety of given representations under the unity of apperception. This principle is the highest in all human cognition."

So, to the *existence* of any *distinguishable object*, there must *pre-exist* the element of mind in the phase of *self*-consciousness as well as *sub*-consciousness. Both must enter the object. Hence, when Kant talked of *"the objective unity of self-consciousness"*—another of his profoundest deductions—he meant literally that "the synthetical unity of apperception," as well as "the synthetical unity of apprehension," is *materialized* in all *conceivable things*. To form the sense-effects of a stone into a single "intuition," they must be merged in a synthesis of apprehension; but to *set* the intuition as thus created—to make it remain *itself* in the midst of *others*, it must be merged with them in a higher synthesis—a common connective consciousness, which, distinguishing them in itself, re-presents them as distinguished.

It was here that Kant reached his famous *"Categories,"* which are merely reflexes of the pure synthetical unity of mind, as forming the unity of all things and of all connection among them.

The principle of mind, beginning, as we have seen, even with the instinctive mind of sense, is a spontaneous self-activity, receptive, reflexive, and resumptive of its doubles. By being the first, it unifies any and every manifold of sense-effects; by being the second, it *re*-presents the product—throws it *out*; by being the third, it apprehends the externalisation, and a percept is born. Apperception, or full consciousness, is the same self-activity, self-reflex, self-sight, transformed into "understanding." Thus, mind is essentially a *triad* as well as a *unit*. But, if so, it must reflect itself to conception as a *"Quantity"*—a sum of its own phases; and in these phases, it is a "Unity," a *"Plurality,"* and a *"Totality."*

Mind, again, as just *a-priori* principle and basis of all things, is manifestly their universal "Quality." But, as self-reflexive, self-resumptive, it is at once a *"Reality,"* a *"Negation,"* and a *"Limitation,"* which means it is that which, in its double, contraposes one state to another, while, as a whole, it is the limit of both states.

It goes without saying that a principle of self-reflex is the "Relation" of its reflexes, and in this relation is a *"Substance* with *Dependence,"* a *"Cause* with *Effect,"* and a *"Reciprocity"* of its separates.

This is a very short cut to the Kantian Categories, but sufficient, perhaps, if we bear in mind that, while *implicit* in the mind of sense, they are reflexes of conscious, not "unconscious" understanding. The synthesis of mind through conceptions proceeds, not by the formation of sense-effects into units of intuition, but by the formation of these already-made units (objects or their properties) into species, genera, and ultimate universals—the pure unity of these groupings, without regard to the things grouped, being just the pure *a priori* unity of self-conscious awareness. Thus, those ultimate universals, the categories, are objective reproductions of pure conceptive synthesis, without which there could be *no connection of things in thought*—which would amount precisely to no *realised objects* and no *objective experience.*

One of Kant's industrious reviewers, Sir William Hamilton, fancied that Aristotle's categories were "genera of real things," while Kant's categories were "determinations of thought," and, as mere *"entia rationis,"* must "be excluded from the Aristotelic list." But there are no "genera of real things" except *as* "determinations of thought"; and, in making an experimental classification of objects, Aristotle found some of the Kantian categories, because the synthetical unity of mind had put those categories into the objects at the creation of them. To Kant an *object* meant something of which Sir William Hamilton had no boding.

CHAPTER XV.

THE GENESIS OF "TRANSCENDENTAL IDEAS."

It must now be easy to see that mind, in its general form, is three-in-one—a triad. It is a self-reflexive, self-related unit, of three phases. The first phase is automatic "apprehension." The second is conscious "understanding." The third, which we touch here, is "reason." In reason, mind is still the general cosmic principle of awareness, with the function of synthesis, or conjunction. As intuition, it has perceived things. As conception, it has classified them. As a last synthetical unity of awareness, it must include, or "comprehend" them—must relate them to its conjunctive unity in their full scope, which means simply in the ultimate reflexes, or forms, of its own nature and action. As process, this can only be done by referring all things to pure synthesis, or connective identity, as *final cause.*

Seeing things, and then *thinking* them, we always end by asking, *"Why?"* They *are*, each and all so and so; but what is the *"reason"* for it? The pure *form* of answer, apart from all contents, is *"because"*—on account of *cause.* Thus reason forms its synthesis of comprehension by referring the particular to the general for a cause—a process that can never stop short of including all things in ultimate unities of cause. It is evident that ultimate unities of cause must contain all subordinate causes or conditions under them. There can be just three such ultimate unities; for there are just three possible kinds of being and conditions that relate to their universals: subjective being and conditions to subjective unity of them; objective being and conditions to objective unity of them; and all being and conditions, both subjective and objective, to the universal unity of being and conditions. These final unities, again, *as* final—as totalities of conditions with none beyond— are themselves "unconditioned."

Reason, then, as an *a-priori* synthetical unity, necessarily refers all conditions of things to their final or absolute unities, which are in reality nothing but conceptional reflexes of Reason's *own constructive* synthetical identity. To *be* an identity of mind, for instance, to the conditions of subjectivity, reason must receive *them* into *its* unity, which thus becomes *their* totality. Now what is the objective re-presentation, the rational conception of the totality of subjective conditions? It is simply the "transcendental idea" of pure subjectiveness, or Soul. In the same way the totality of objective phenomenal conditions, is the idea of the Universe; while the totality of *all* conditions, both subjective and objective, is the idea of that in which all mind and all matter are related as their final cause or reason—God.

CHAPTER XVI.
THE GRAND RESULT OF DISSECTING PHENOMENA.

Since the days of Immanuel Kant, no philosophy, no rational theology, no ultimate science, not referring to the results of his work, has had any real basis in thought—the reason being that he saw through, and explained, the principle of universal relativity, the law of scientific idealism, and relaid the whole structure, from the corner-stone up.

Before Kant it was known well enough that "matter," however we must all accept it with our hands and eyes, has no standing, under the analysis of thought, except as a system of effects on ourselves. Hume, we remember, saw all this so clearly that he pronounced the very organs of sense, "our limbs and members," to be "not our body," but "certain impressions" to which the mind ascribes "a corporeal existence." Our limbs and members certainly *are* our body—the only body we have—but Hume was right in his meaning that our body is a phenomenon which has no existence but as a plexus of impressions on a principle of intelligence, possessing various modes of reception, named senses. But this *principle* of *intelligence* itself was, to Hume, not a fact to be grasped by "reason," not a principle to be known and described, but was to be taken as a "force and vivacity" unknowable beyond an *instinct* of it. Hume's unknowable "force and vivacity"—an improved form of Locke's "blank-tablet"—Kant *analyzed* in the light of its products; namely, those conjuncts of sense-effects called objects; those conjuncts of objects called species, genera, and categories; and finally those conjuncts of all things and all conditions of things, called transcendental ideas. Now, such conjuncts of various "manifolds" actually exist. They are man's percepts and concepts; they are his facts, his environment. But *as* percepts and concepts, and always conjuncts of "the manifold," they are formed, organized, totalized, through a *principle*—the principle of perception and conception itself. This is Kant's *a-priori* synthetical unit, common and necessary to all "things" and to all "experience."

The last word of any weight, against this reduction of matter to mind, was said a few years ago by that exceptionally acute thinker, Professor Huxley, in his summary of Hume. Too able and learned, both as philosopher and scientist, to question idealism, Huxley admitted it unqualifiedly. But, not having gone beyond the British proofs of it, he defended what is commonly called "materialism" in this way:

"If we analyze the proposition that all mental phenomena are the effects or products of material phenomena, all that it means amounts to this: that whenever those states of consciousness which we call sensation, or emotion, or thought, come into existence, complete investigation will show good reason for the belief that they are preceded by those other phenomena of consciousness to which we give the names of matter and motion. All material changes appear, in the long run, to be modes of motion; but our knowledge of motion is nothing but that of a change in the place and order of our sensations; just as our knowledge of matter is restricted to those feelings of which we assume it to be the cause."

To this last posture of materialism, a competent understanding of Kant is the *only reply that has ever been needed*. It is simply of no consequence to the case what states of consciousness precede or follow other states of consciousness. Let it be granted (whether true or not) that "phenomena of consciousness to which we give the names of matter and motion" precede all others. What of it? Kant has proved to us that *no* phenomenon of consciousness—no matter, no motion, no sensation—and, beyond all these, no time and no space, in which all the rest appear—has, or can have, *any existence*, except as put into unity, form, and order, by the unity, form, and order of mind. If both "the synthesis of apprehension" and "the synthesis of apperception" enter into any state of consciousness named matter, *to give it birth*, there is no possibility that the element of intelligence can be an *after-birth* of the process.

All our objects, then, from a germ cell to the horizon, are constructed such through a mental principle innate in our own structure. But here it must be re-iterated and re-emphasized that whatever we, as units of mind, may embody in objects as *form*, the *filling* of them is not ours. It has a source apart. The filling of our objects comes from "the ultimate non-ego," the "background of matter." This ultimate non-ego was a heritage to Kant from British idealism. He took it for granted at his first step and held by it unchanged when he was old and exhausted. He called it the "noumenon," the "real correlate of matter," and pluralized it as "things in themselves." But he insisted, as firmly as Herbert Spencer has since done, that the "noumenon" is "unknown and unknowable."

In a certain way—vital enough, too—"things in themselves" *are* "unknown and unknowable." Man is a small, dependent, limited being. Let us admit at once every old proverb in the world, to the effect that "the finite cannot comprehend the infinite." Sir William Hamilton issued a tedious list of such proverbs. Let us adopt the whole of it. "The finite cannot comprehend the infinite." The very meaning of "things in themselves" is that they are withheld from us in their *specific contents*. But in their *general nature* they are related and revealed to us; and the revelation is always asserted when we name them "source of impact," the "real correlate of matter," "things in themselves," or even "the unknown and unknowable." Is there an "unknown and unknowable?" Yes, there *is*. But whatever *is* has *being*—*must* have being, or not be that which "is." So much then we *know* of "the unknown and unknowable"; it has being; it is a *fact*. But we know it negatively, as well as positively. We know what it is *not*, on precisely the same ground that we know what it *is*. Being a "noumenon," it is *not* a phenomenon; being a "thing in *itself*," it is not what things are to *us*. Being "the real correlate of matter," it is *not* matter, but is the objective background of matter.

But *now*: Kant had analyzed matter and found it to be a *relation*—a relation between finite subjective awareness and this very noumenal background now in evidence. He had found, too, that all *matter*—every spicule of it—is *exhausted in the relation*. He had found that, out of the relation, *matter has no existence*. By these presents, then, we know that the objective background of matter, the ultimate non-ego, is *not material*.

And, at this point, where are we, if we pause and think? When reduced to elements, to principles, what is there of the universe—the all of things? Just the subjective and the objective, mind and matter. Hence, that which is *not matter* is *mind*. Nothing else is left for it.

We may wriggle at this terminus as much as we like, but there is no dodging it. It may be said, for instance, that, while we *know* and *experience* nothing but mind and matter (including with matter its phenomenal vistas, space and time), we can *imagine something* else than either; and, during the past fifty years, this nonsense has found lodgment in some heads. Now I can imagine *anything*, in the meaning that I can arbitrarily produce some foolish *fancy*. I can imagine a white blackbird, with his tail-feathers on his head. But I cannot imagine even this self-evident contradiction as a thing of neither mind nor matter. What is an object of "imagination" in the meaning of fancy? It may be empty of matter, and so unlike the white blackbird. But *no* object of imagination can be empty of mind. Imagination is itself an act of mind; hence every possible product of imagination must partake of mind. If, therefore, I imagine something apart from mind and matter, it must still spring from mind, contain mind, and so *not* be apart from mind. The *"reductio ad absurdum"* can be had cheap and sure, just where it is most needed.

After Immanuel Kant had once and for good dissected the universe, it seems a pity that he declined to put his findings together, and take the last logical step of his magnificent demonstrations. As a requisite, perhaps, to his microscopic analysis of human subjectivity, he declined to generalize his own discoveries. In short, Kant's synthesis was Hegel. But Hegel we need not follow, as our short cut to him, through the solution of noumena, is worth more, as yet, than the whole German tour of "post-Kantean philosophy."

Very early in his work Kant said:

"There are two sources of human knowledge (which probably spring from *a common, but to us unknown root*), namely, sense and understanding. By the former, objects are *given* to us; by the latter, *thought*."

Dissecting, with Kant, the nature of "understanding," we have discovered in it the unal form of all our re-presentations—of every perceptible and conceivable objected fact. Dissecting "sense," with the same instructor, we have found it to be certain modes of mental susceptibility, its physical organs being nothing but relations between susceptible awareness and the noumenal unknown, like all the rest of "matter." Led, once more, by our Professor straight up to this noumenal unknown, where *he* willed to stop and turn his back on it, we have only had to *look*, in order to see it collapse into the self-retention of Spirit—spirit *out* of *us*, but still *in itself*, and thus going to make up the totality of Spiritual Being. We have thus found the "one common root" of all knowledge and all things. But we have touched, also, the apex of thought, and can now see what is meant—really and fully meant—by "*absolute idealism.*"

Absolute Idealism is not merely a phrase; it is a grand and glorious fact. Immersed in matter, stuck in our senses, we may insist on looking at sensuous phenomena as our friend John Jasper looked at the sun, with honest contempt for Copernicus and Newton. "De earf do *not* move roun' de sun," exclaimed the sturdy preacher, "but de bressed sun move roun' de earf. Dere she go now: don't I see her wi' dese very eyes?" Parson Jasper did see the sun moving round the earth, and in the same way we all see the objects of our senses existing in perfect independence of ourselves. Still, as surely as astronomy has proved the delusion of taking the sun's movement from the eye, philosophy, with the aid of "practical science," has proved the delusion of taking objective re-presentations as not constructed through subjective being. The inevitable end of this proof is the dissolution of noumena as anything "material," and the inclusion of all things in Universal Spirit. Of such spirit, finite subjectivity is a function—a necessary participative reflex, through which the Universal Spirit is life, manifestation, self-evolution.

CHAPTER XVII.

SOME SEQUENCES OF ABSOLUTE IDEALISM.

Since Kant, we have said, "no philosophy, no rational theology, no ultimate science, not referring to the results of his work, has had any real basis in thought." It must be added that since the fulfilment of Kant's *Critique*, especially by Hegel, there has not been one stone left as a foundation for "materialism." It goes right on, however, in multifarious forms, its defunct exponents still imagining they live. Surgical psychology, in special, is still as active with scalpel and microscope as if ours were the day of Coudillac and Erasmus Darwin. The knife goes into the brain, and the eye peers after it, with the funny expectation of seeing, with Dr. Cabanis, some spicule or plexus of matter, there, "which secretes thought as the liver secretes bile." The work is excellent as anatomy, and may have a plenty of important uses. But we, here, if we have had the capacity and patience to grasp the findings of Immanuel Kant, know that mind can never be derived from any physical correspondence of its nature and action. We know that every possible attempt at such derivation is merely a side-show of Parson Jasper's great astronomical comedy, which Copernicus exploded four hundred years ago. We know that every fiber, every solid or liquid, of the brain, with every movement of every atom it contains, is a ready-made physical object in a ready-made space and a ready-made time. But if we know Kant, we know, without a misgiving, that space and time, with all things in them, are not only dependencies but are literal creations and manufactures of a universal principle named *mind*. We know it is this principle which furnishes the form, the unity, and so the very existence of every phenomenon. Hence we know, finally, that the first step in the understanding of matter is the analysis of mind, through which all matter *is* and is *constructed*. Without this first step, all other steps are simply a stumble in the dark—the blind-man's buff of children. Or we may say, with a little more dignity, perhaps, that every material law of the cosmos is subject to "The Law of Scientific Idealism."

Now scientific idealism, pursued to the end, merges in absolute idealism. The source and substance of the universe is Intelligent Spirit; or, as the Bible and its Theologians say, this is the All-In-All.

For fifty years—from the publication of Kant's *Critique* in 1781, along through Fichte, and Schelling, to the death of Hegel in 1831—the vast illumination of thought that has been summed up as "German Transcendentalism" strove to unify natural theology and practical science in "Absolute Idealism." It will yet be seen that the work was done, however ill-comprehended. The good old Kant still had his whole head with him when he said, in 1787, "the danger, in this case, is not that of being refuted, but of being misunderstood." The Comtes, the Hamiltons, the Mills and Spencers—with no end, too, of their German brothers—are illustrious examples in proof of Kant's remark, however greatly they may be respected within the limits of their own work.

Once and for good, the history of philosophy, when understood, and the history of science, when understood, have joined in the proof that the principle of all life—we may say God if we like—is Spirit Principle.

Transcendentalism—a bulky word, but covering much more than the letter of it—was naturally too high and too deep a result to get all at once into the average human head. For thirty-odd years after the close of its epoch in Germany—or until, in 1864, Dr. James Hutchison Stirling produced his *Secret of Hegel*—not a man stood on the earth adequate to reproduce transcendentalism in basis and system. But the practical gist of it, without the full center or circumference, gradually became a part of the world's literature. In Britain, most notably through Thomas Carlyle, the new light penetrated biography, history, criticism, and even political disquisition. In America, focused in Ralph Waldo Emerson, the same light, whiter and purer if less flaming and burning, both vivified and purified all things on which it was shed. There the Infinite Oversoul and the finite undersoul seemed once again to meet in communion and evolution. Meanwhile, Theodore Parker, with his vast scholarship and overpowering courage, preached Jesus of Nazareth, the Sermon on the Mount, and the Golden Rule, with little regard for any organized theology of his day, whether its Unitarianism or its Calvinistic Orthodoxy. Back of all this, as now appears, there was a plain, uncultured, but inquiring and thoughtful man, in the byways of New England, who from the mechanism of clocks turned to the workings of the human mind, and in his own way reached the depth of knowledge and the mysteries of life. From a few practical experiments, he, too, analyzed the things of matter, and found them to be re-presentations, externalizations, of elemental spirit. And then he drew the inference that spirit molds, directs, governs matter, and so that health of mind materializes health of body.

But now, at once, the whole question at issue confronts us—what is the true and full position and power *of mind in therapeutics*? This question must be answered, here, not from the Quimby standpoint, and much less from that of the shallow muddle termed Christian Science, but from the standpoint of actual, accredited, established metaphysics, now substantially bearing the concensus of religion, philosophy, and the practical investigation of material phenomena.

By aid of Kant, with our short-cut to the logical and necessary end of his achievement, we have grasped the elemental source and solvent of man and his universe. It is Spirit in its evolution. But, in this evolution, man—or say rather and always *the principle of sensation and consciousness in which man inheres*—is merely the general form, diversely individualized, of the One All-Inclusive Spirit in the activity of self-manifestation. The earth, the sun, moon, and stars, the human body, its house and the landscape, with every particle of all of them, are outwoven of universal Spirit through the loom of subjective being and unity. The forms of matter, with no exception, are fabricated in this way. Thus, not figuratively, but literally and with exact knowledge, we may repeat after St. John:

"In the beginning was the Word, and the Word was with God, and the Word was God. All things were made by him; and without him was not anything made that was made."

But the principle of animal apprehension and human apperception—or say just the conscious and the sub-conscious—is not the Ultimately Creative One, but is, in *us*, only a sub-creative power and agency. We simply individualize it in endless degrees and variations, all of us framing the same general world of objects, conceptions and feelings, but no one of us being, seeing, or feeling, in all respects, exactly like any other incarnation of our common identity.

But while the *form*—the unity, and thus the individuality—of all things, is materialized from Spirit through sensation and consciousness in subjectivity—while this is the secret and genesis of all creation—we must ever hold fast to the equally basic and universal fact that the *filling* of the form—the infinite variety of impact on subjectivity which furnishes the diversity of objects—all this comes from that ultimate spirit-background crudely called "the unknown and unknowable."

Now this background of Absolute Spirit, the very withholding of which from finite creatures constitutes them such, institutes their law of progress, and gives movement of expression to the Infinite Itself, can only be absorbed and mastered by human beings through study, work, and experience. While genuine metaphysics, then, assures us of our spirit-origin and relative oneness with God—of being God's children far more directly and intimately than most of us have ever imagined—it teaches us that for practical purposes, in our condition of existence called "matter," it makes no difference *what* we *call* this condition. 'Tis something actual, something definite, something *fixed*, just as long as we are in our earthly relation to it. From this point of view, Dr. Johnson's kicking of the stone to refute Berkeley was a deserved kick, and even Byron's fun was justified in his tipsy lines,

> "When Bishop Berkeley said there was no matter,
> And proved it, 'twas no matter what he said."

All things are spirit surely enough; but the phenomena of matter, as transformed spirit, are related to each other under the laws of what we necessarily designate as material nature. Little by little, through long and hard exertion, we find out what these relations are, and how they are fitted to the human center of them. Some things are good to eat and to nourish us; others to poison and kill us. A cold or fever may be a manifestation of spirit, and an herb or drug may be another; but if the herb or drug counteracts and destroys the cold or the fever, and experience proves it ten thousand times, who cares to analyze a dose of aconite or a cup of saffron-tea into a draft of "mortal" or "immortal" mind? The process is a mere fooling with ideals—hysterics jumping at the moon. *On metaphysical grounds*—as far as anybody knows what metaphysics really means—there is no need that our physicians, if they are "good physicians," should trouble themselves much about a Mrs. Mary Baker G. Eddy. Esculapius came into the world long before her, and his followers will stay in it long after her materialized divinity has risen into a more spiritual and a more intelligent state.

The same may be said of our theologians. Their creeds have not come out of nothing, however much the spirit of them may have grown thick and muddy through crude understandings. The Christian Church, surely, can yet offer to mankind something better than the Eddy "Church Scientist"; and if it can, it is in no ultimate jeopardy from a few, or a few hundred, congregations of half-educated faddists.

For a student of history—not in its moments, but in its decades and centuries—it is easy to see that "Christian Science" has the reason of the fact and *the spread of it*, in its being a protest against the depressing materialism around it—a materialism which, though rationally decapitated by Kant, has shown marvelous activity, for a corpse, ever since the execution.

The medical profession, too, has partly, if indirectly, been responsible for Mrs. Eddy's crazy horse of "metaphysics," running away in the dark, and butting its own brains out. From Dr. Mesmer to Dr. Charcot, it took about a hundred and twenty years for "animal magnetism," under the softer names of "hypnotism" and "suggestion," to achieve full and final standing in the French Academy of Medicine; and the mental phenomena attending "mesmerism" have still but little "respectability" among "regular physicians." But, that curative agencies are not confined to drugs has long been settled in the public mind—such part of the public mind, at least, as permits itself any considerable reading and thinking.

Has the pulpit itself—orthodox and not so orthodox—contributed to the success of Eddy "Science"? We must say it has. The practise, among the sects, of twisting the Bible out of its straight, historical, natural significance, and fitting its texts to every sort of whim, folly, and malefaction—this general practise has at last culminated in Mrs. Eddy's *Key to the Scriptures*, with pretty nearly the dissolution of them in the abomination of interpretation.

But "Christian Science"—the Eddy misfit for a specious name—has had its rise, and it has probably risen about as high as it can reach, notwithstanding its rapid extension for the moment. Only its protrusion from insignificance and non-attention was needed to uncover its foundation on the sands of ignorance, its strength in the perennial weakness and credulity of mankind, and its business success in ordinary, or more than ordinary, business cupidity. Has it done no good in the world, then? Ah, that is another question. Whatever may have been the chief motive of its founder, and whatever may have been its "comedy of errors," it has forced the inception of a movement that, as a whole, may have vast results for the human mind and the human body. Whatever material medicines may be necessary to mankind while they themselves are in a material condition, psychic forces in the cure of disease can no longer be ignored. What is the extent, and what the limit, of these forces, is a problem that must be examined. As conditionally—here and now—man is *both spiritual and corporeal*—it would seem to be a self-evident conclusion that he must have both material and spiritual aids to health. That we can "jump" our condition, before we get out of it, is the most tremendous paradox ever presented to the human mind; but the sequences—even physical—of systematically opening the finite soul to the Infinite Spirit may be incalculable. The revival, or definite rediscovery, in modern times, of healing the sick by the soul and the laying-on of hands, came to pass some fifty years ago, in the United

States, through the honest, single-minded, Phineas Parkhurst Quimby. If the spirit of evil—of hypocrisy, selfishness and avarice—has entered into the movement of mental healing through another source, the frequent necessity of very human means to divine ends is once more illustrated.

CHAPTER XVIII.

VARIOUS SCHOOLS OF THE NEW THOUGHT.

Just now, the general cause of metaphysical therapeutics is separating rapidly into various "schools," few of them having much consideration for the pretentious health-trust, "Christian Science."

In the South, for instance—at Sea Breeze, Florida—a Mrs. Helen Wilmans has founded a settlement of houses and lands, souls and bodies, with books, pamphlets, and a weekly press, all devoted, mentally, morally and physically, to psychic dominion over all things. *Freedom* is the name of the organ that specially spreads Mrs. Wilmans' light and curatives. She has capacity in a comparative degree, and energy, with self-confidence, in the superlative. She proclaims this:

"Intellectual power in the individual comes from concentration of the mind upon an idea until the truth or falsity of the idea becomes apparent. Likewise the power of the race in the unfoldment of a race problem must come from a concentrated effort to discover a hitherto unfolded racial capacity; and this is the meaning of the movement I am inaugurating here."

The Wilmans' conception of mind-healing has been illustrated as follows by a correspondent of *Freedom*, who discusses and admits the curing of disease among devout Catholics, exalted and prayerful, at the shrine of St. Anne in Illinois. It is all natural, he says:

"If with equally strong belief they should pray to God, Buddha, St. Peter or Paul, Mrs. Eddy or Mrs. Wilmans, or a stump or stone—or should they stand on their heads, or drink water from a certain river, or anoint the sick parts with clay and spittle—the result would be the same. Their mind would cure their bodies. Mind is king."

In some respects, the paper, *Freedom*, is almost as free from "material sense" as the book, *Science and Health*. Mrs. Wilmans has a correspondent who asserts, and probably believes, that, by the concentrated power of her finite female mind, she has "never failed once in five years to avert the fury of severe summer storms." She has "demonstrated," she says, the dominion of mind over material nature, "as clearly as any Mental Scientist has demonstrated it over disease."

And here is an official announcement from Mrs. Wilmans' organ:

"*Freedom* is the only paper published whose leading and constantly avowed object is to overcome death right here in this world and right now. If you want to learn something of the newly-discovered power vested in man which fits him for this stupendous conquest, read this paper, and keep on reading it."

"The new thought" has traveled West as far as South. It recently had among its organs *The Temple*, of Denver, Colorado, "a monthly magazine devoted to the fuller unfoldment of the divinity of humanity," the editor of which was Mr. Paul Tyner, who afterwards conducted the *Arena* of Boston, consolidated with *The Journal of Practical Metaphysics*. The purpose of the latter periodical was "the unification of scientific and spiritual thought and the new philosophy of health." The editor was Horatio W. Dresser, a Harvard graduate, an excellent philosopher of the ontological trend, and a polished writer, reminding one partly of Spinoza and partly of Emerson. Mr. Dresser's books, *The Power of Silence*, *The Perfect Whole*, and others, have given him a wide reputation in his particular field of work, and have constituted him a center of the most logical and scholarly literature connected with "metaphysical healing." This literature, too extensive for specialized designation, is under the propagandism of the Boston "Metaphysical Club," an active and growing organization.

The Boston "Metaphysical Club" comprises too much exact information and solid learning to accept or countenance the extreme vagaries of "Christian Science," and appears to be acting as a balance-wheel to the whole movement of "the new thought." In a recent leaflet the Club has taken special occasion to dissect and repudiate that most preposterous doctrine of Mrs. Eddy's "science," the absolute nothingness of matter.

The title of the leaflet referred to is *Christian Science and the New Metaphysical Movement*, with the added phrase, *An Intelligent Discrimination Desirable*. One excerpt is this:

"Christian Science proclaims the unreality of matter, and of the body. The rational and broader thought, not only admits the validity of the body, as veritable expression, but claims that it is as good, in its own place and plane, as is the soul and spirit. While susceptible to mental molding, it is neither an error nor an illusion. Moreover, it is friendly to its welfare to affirm both its validity and goodness. It is to be ruled, beautified, and utilized in its own order, and not denied an existence. Even admitting that the whole cosmos is, in the last analysis, but one Universal Mind and its manifestation; even admitting that all matter is but a lower vibration of spirit, and that the human body is essentially a mental rather than a physical organism; still, matter has its own relative reality and validity, and is not to be ignored as illusion."

Of its kind, nothing better than this could be said even by a Hegel. It is exactly the correct statement of the great metaphysical truth.

The leaflet agrees with the criticism of this volume, that "the spirit of Christian Science is autocratic rather than democratic," and says:

"Its polity and ritual, in every detail, are shaped and directed arbitrarily by a single will. There is no room for investigation, liberty of thought, progress, or further revelation. There is no recognition of related physical science or evolutionary progress."

The monograph continues thus:

"The liberal movement stands for freedom of soul, and is in no way opposed to subordinate orders of truth.... It does not ignore the good in existing systems, disparage reasonable hygiene, or deny the place of certain departments of surgery. It is not insensible to the present and provisional uses of simple external therapeutic agencies, at least until individual unfoldment and the recognition of higher law become more general.... While understanding, both from experience and observation, that a systematic employment of mental potency in a rational, scientific, and idealistic manner has a wonderful and unappreciated healing energy, its exponents do not think it necessary to form a new and exclusive religious sect."

The main premise, of course, of all the schools of "mind-healing" is that "the mind can and should control the body." Let us go straight from this premise to the manner of applying it, as explained, for instance, in a little book entitled *The New Philosophy of Health*, excellently well written, by a Miss Harriet B. Bradbury.

"The healer [says this author] simply holds in mind with great tenacity, for perhaps ten or fifteen minutes, an image of the patient as he should be. This image, by the process known as 'thought transference' is impressed upon the sick man's mind as a possibility, when his own strong desire, seizing it, is able to reproduce it as an actuality. He may be quite unconscious that he has done anything for himself, and when he finds himself well, gives all the credit to the man who, as he thinks, has 'healed' him. Yet the change is wrought by no man, but by the great life-giving force which two wills working in harmony have called into perfect action."

In confirmation of "the law of mental causation," Miss Bradbury says:

"The most significant of recent biological experiments are those which have been conducted at the Smithsonian Institute with a view to discovering the physical effects of different mental states. They have proved that the different emotions produce immediate chemical changes within the physical organism, and it only remains to continue the investigation to learn just how each habitual emotion is finally reflected upon the outward frame."

So that "old mesmerist," Dr. Quimby—for this was exactly his view—has got along as far as the Smithsonian Institute at Washington. And here let us introduce the names and cogitations of a few authorities so "eminently respectable" that the "very best and most conservative people" need not shrink from becoming acquainted with them.

In a work on *Practical Idealism*, William DeWitt Hyde, President of Bowdoin College, tells us:

"There are certain classes of disease for which hypnotic treatment is highly beneficial. Mental healing in all its various forms, in so far as it is valuable, rests on the principle that body and mind are very closely inter-related through the partly conscious but chiefly unconscious control of the vital functions through the nervous system; and that the state of the mind at any given time, and consequently the state of the body, in so far as we know it at that time, is made up of a relatively small presentation of sensation, and a very large contribution of associations. Hence a very slight suggestion through the senses, by speech, or physical contact, or eradication of fixed images, anxieties, and fears, may introduce a new nucleus around which an entirely new set of associations will cluster; so that through the renewing of the mind the body may come to be transformed."

Charles Van Norden, D.D., LL.D., at one time President of Elmira College, tells us in his outline of psychology, *The Psychic Factor*, that

> "So tremendous is this power of mind over body, that disease may often be cured and ailments caused by a new idea."

> "A woman [says Rev. Dr. Van Orden] once came to Surgeon-General Hammond with what he considered an incurable disorder. She sighed as she turned to go away disconsolate, saying, 'Ah, if I but had some of the water of Lourdes!' — for she was a devout Catholic. Now it so happened that a friend had brought the doctor a bottle of the genuine water of Lourdes to experiment with. He informed the patient of this, and promised her some provided she would first try a more potent remedy, Aqua Crotonis (New York City aqueduct water). The woman consented, but protesting that this latter could not reach the case. He then gave her a little vial of the real article, but labeled 'Aqua Crotonis.' When this had failed he gave her Croton water, but labeled 'Water of Lourdes.' The result was a complete cure."

Prof. William James, of Harvard, in the chapter of his *Principles of Psychology* treating "the production of movement," quotes many authorities and gives various diagrams illustrating the effects of sensations and emotions upon the pulse, the respiration, the glands, muscles, and other organs and functions of men and animals. The celebrated Prof. Bain is quoted as saying that "according as an impression is accompanied with *feeling*, the aroused currents diffuse themselves over the brain, leading to a general agitation of the moving organs, as well as affecting the viscera." The conclusion of Prof. James is that

> "Using sweeping terms and ignoring exceptions, we might say that every possible feeling produces a movement, and that every movement is a movement of the entire organism, and of each and all its parts."

"The effect," says Prof. James, "of fear, shame and anger, upon the blood-supply of the skin, especially the skin of the face, are too well known to need remark. Sensations of the higher senses produce, according to Couty and Charpentier, the most varied effects upon the pulse-rate and blood-pressure of dogs."

Now if the higher emotions of dogs produce marked effects upon their physical structure, we must naturally infer that hope, faith, joy — all, indeed, of the loftier emotions of human beings — may set up high and healthful movements in the human body, while base emotions set up low, harmful, and diseased conditions. In this claim, anyhow, we have, according to "metaphysical healing," the cause and cure of disease, capped, too, with the ethics of "the new thought."

Thomas Jay Hudson, in his book, *The Law of Psychic Phenomena*, gives this compend of the facts:

"The science of psycho-therapeutics is yet in its infancy. Thus far just enough has been learned to stimulate research. It has been demonstrated that there is a psychic power inherent in man which can be employed for the amelioration of his own physical condition, as well as that of his fellows. When this is said, nearly all the ground covered by present knowledge has been embraced. It is true that many wonderful cures have been effected, many marvelous phenomena developed. Nevertheless, all are groping in the dark, with only an occasional glimmering of distant light shed upon the subject; and this light serves principally to show how little is now known, compared with what there is yet to learn."

In discussing the conditions necessary to psychic healing, Mr. Hudson affirms that the exemplar and healer of Nazareth, the founder of our Christian religion, always recognized these conditions in the "miracles" imputed to him. We shall end our quotations, at this point, with one from Mr. Hudson's chapter on "The Physical Manifestations and Philosophy of Christ."

"I do not mean to say that Jesus could not heal in such cases where the mental environment was unfavorable; but the fact that he took infinite pains, wherever practicable, to secure the best conditions, shows that he understood the law and worked within its limitations. Certain it is that he never performed any of his wonderful works outside the laws which he proclaimed, nor did he ever intimate that he could do so. It is true that his biographers do not always relate the details of the transactions recorded; but it must be remembered that they wrote at a later day, and may not have been in possession of all the details. It is, however, a marvelous fact, and is one which constitutes indubitable evidence of the truth of his history, that in no instance do they relate a single act performed or word spoken by him, relating to the healing of the sick, which does not reveal his perfect knowledge of and compliance with the laws which pertain to mental therapeutics as they are revealed in modern times through experiment and the processes of inductive reasoning."

CHAPTER XIX.

AN ADVANCED HEALER OF TO-DAY.

Recapitulating what we have been over, it appears that "metaphysical healing" is simply the suggestion and determination of health—the ideal photograph, as it were, of health—transferred from the well to the ill, in the conviction that Universal Spirit is the principle of all health, which we may receive from its Source by opening ourselves to it. That is to say, the health of the Infinite Spirit, so far as absorbed by a finite spirit, corrects finite errors of mind, and the mind, thus corrected, corrects, or cures, the body. Such, certainly, was the "truth-cure" of Phineas P. Quimby. With him, starting as a mesmerist, it was, really, a kind of normal and sacred hypnotism, by which he endeavored to put his patients under the close, immediate influence and operation of Supreme Life, and Sympathy, and Vigor.

Such treatment should do much for the ailing—how much we must wait to know.

But the effects of it must have limits, and these limits must be the general, the fixed conditions, of what we designate as mind and matter. It may be well to restate these conditions, but with focal reference to this point—the one vital point of our whole theme.

Metaphysically speaking, we are spirit, and all else is spirit. But what *is* spirit? What are the constituents of it, to the extent that man may grasp them?

First, is the universal principle of intelligent conjunctive unity, instinctive and conscious, which, individualized in men and animals, manufactures, or sub-creates, all the unities of their environment, which they take to be "the forms of matter."

Second, is the equally universal principle of subjective (negative) sensibility— the receptiveness of spirit in its forms called "the senses." Transmuted through these senses, ultimate objective spirit—to us "the unknown and unknowable"— furnishes the filling, or contents, of what consciousness and sub-consciousness make up, or unify, into objects.

Third, is the vast fact of Spirit-background—Infinite Spirit "in itself"—which is revealed, and can only be revealed, *to the finite*, as transformed through fixed modes of finite receptivity.

A man, therefore, is simply an individualization of the process by which the Absolute—That Which Is—expresses itself and lives. Whatever may be our environment under some changed state of our receptivity—say "the future life"—our environment of spirit objected through sense, in space and time, is the environment of *matter*; and the human body is a part of it. We are not only "in matter," therefore, but we sub-create the matter, through our God-given modes of sensuous receptivity, and can only escape from it through an entire change of those modes, called "senses." The door of escape is the door of death, and no human being has ever avoided it. *Can* any human being avoid it? We say *no*: because to be out of matter is to be out of the kind of receptiveness—our five senses—through which matter itself exists. If there be exceptional persons of clairvoyant susceptibility, who can pass sufficiently out of our average material condition to realize aught beyond them, the *bodily* state of these persons, too, must end, as we all end.

Let us not mix conditions, like the metaphysical tyros of Christian Science; but while we are in the state of spirit known and experienced as mind *and* matter, let us acknowledge the plain fact. As a corollary of this fact, if we are out of health, let us look to remedies good for *both mind and matter*—the body and the soul. Such will probably be the ultimate equipoise between "mental medicine" and material curatives.

This, at any rate, is the best conclusion for "the new thought" that the scribe at hand can reach. He may be wrong; for he is totally "uninspired," and has nothing to follow but his nose and his "mortal mind." But, the conclusion once reached, he stood on it as an *a-priori* breathing-spot. And then it occurred to him that, peradventure, some radical, independent son of Galen might be conducting the business of therapeutics on a psycho-corporeal, double platform. If so, Boston would be the place to look for him, and the search was begun. In due time it was successful. The result may at least prove suggestive and entertaining.

Let our new friend be called Prof. P.; for he has been an instructor in his kind of work, and he bears the title of "doctor" only by the courtesy of his patients, as Dr. Quimby did.

Now it is certain that if Prof. P. does not cure all sorts of diseases, his patients think he does, vouch for it when questioned, and give most sincere testimonials to that effect. Even the cure of cancer is vigorously affirmed, and in connection with cases that have been given up by eminent physicians. But, as this book is doing no medical advertising, one ordinary instance of Prof. P.'s work must suffice.

A large, strong woman, as the consequence of a fall, incurred violent sciatic rheumatism, and was treated at a hospital for three months, being worse at the end of that time than at first. On personally interviewing her—and she is a woman of more than average intelligence—she informed the writer that, in one treatment of twenty minutes, Prof. P. had "entirely cured" her, and that after five months— which had elapsed at the time of the conversation—there had been no recurrence of her trouble.

Our search for light has led to a somewhat close acquaintance with Prof. P. and has induced him to explain his theory and practise of healing, for our use as a writer, excepting a few of his personal discoveries not immediately important to the public, which he must withhold, he says, for something like the same reason that his learned brothers, the physicians, write their prescriptions in Latin.

Prof. P. requires it to be said explicitly that he is a Spiritualist. He is so pronounced in the faith that he impatiently scoffs at all denial, evasion or concealment, of what he deems his "positive knowledge" that we exist after "our mere change of condition called death," and that "the spirits of our departed friends are interested in our earthly welfare." He declares, however, that Dr. Quimby was sensible in not trusting spirit communications at the expense of his own judgment—"as, taking the long generations of mankind, there are necessarily more fools disembodied than in the flesh."

According to our friend P., there are now four great remedial agencies possible to healing the sick, apart from medicines in the usual sense. The intelligent and careful use of such medicines he believes in, and he seeks to cooperate with all broad-minded physicians, rather than to antagonize them. The more occult, but often more effective agencies, than drugs or herbs, he says, are these:

First: Animal Magnetism.

Second: Natural Healing-Power—this power being inherent to some extent in all human beings, but greatly concentrated and developed in certain individuals.

Third: Mental or Psychic Force—a force existing in both embodied and disembodied spirits, and as a universal principle.

Fourth: "Sensitized" devices containing these powers and elements, with the function of imparting them to the ailing and the weary.

"Magnetism," says our Professor, "as a material phenomenon, is a force so potent that it rearranges the unsystematized molecules of certain metals, and gives them harmonious direction and integral traction. The application of it—termed polarization—has been known even to produce 'clicks' within metallic bodies, loud enough to be distinctly heard. Animal magnetism, pertaining to organized beings, acts upon their corresponding but higher molecules in the same general way. The sick are disordered, locally clogged, 'out of tune.' They have lost, as it were, their polarity. Animal magnetism restores it to them. It then goes further and vitalizes them; for, if imparted to the feeble by a person strong, well, and stored full of it, an equilibrium takes place between an operator and his patient. Animal magnetism, however unconsciously utilized, doubtless takes part in all so-called 'mind-cures' that are *physical* afflictions, not the results of bugaboos and whimsies. The absurd fulminations of Mrs. Eddy, at this late day, against animal magnetism, are only equaled by the comprehensive ignorance, in general, which Bishop Brooks is said to have considered the only possible excuse for the production of a book like *Science and Health*.

"Inherent Healing Power is more occult than animal magnetism, but has become almost as well established. According to the accepted evidence of centuries, this power was fully exemplified in ancient times by the most faithful and unselfish of all the sons of God and man, Jesus, our Christ. According to recent and contemporary evidence, both widespread and exact, the Protestant world of late centuries has had no example of the same quality so marked as that of Dr. P. P. Quimby. Inherent healing power goes with close and tender sympathy for the afflicted, and grows with use, like the brawn of a stevedore, or the intellectual dexterity of a practised writer. It may eventuate in a Quimby as naturally as the poetic faculty eventuates in a Kipling.

"By mental or psychic force," says the Professor, "I mean the principle of apprehending, understanding, and reasoning, with the moral elements pertaining to conscience and will. This combination of our essential being, in whatever phase of it we may exist, affects and modifies, if it does not altogether dominate, all the rest of our make-up. Its importance is very great, but may be exaggerated by forgetting that man is a microcosm, and that while he is in the externalized condition of spirit known as matter he is not at the same time *out* of it. For the finite to put itself in harmony with the Infinite, by right thinking, right feeling, right conduct, is indispensable to the highest health; but an imaginary union with God through fictitious conceptions of our own ego is unnatural and unwholesome exaltation, inducing disease of the mind, whatever it may do to the body.

"Psychic power is an absolutely universal principle, common, in degree, to men, spirits, and God. It is sometimes employed by hypnotists to such an extent that the physical sensation of a subject is rendered void, even under amputation of a bodily member. It can destroy the taste for intoxicants in a drunkard. It can supplant melancholia with hope and cheerfulness. What it can *not* do is yet a problem.

"Of course such a power is a part, and great part, of sane therapeutics. In the application of it," said the Professor, with much warmth, "I affirm—let those who have not my knowledge and experience think what their ignorance or prejudice saddles upon them—that 'departed spirits,' as we call them, combine their efforts with those of men and women, to heal the sick. The power is thus redoubled.

"We have taken but a few steps in this sort of knowledge, and it is accompanied by a plenty of deception and twaddle. But the truth underlying it has now procured a hearing even before eminently timid 'societies of psychical research,' and will soon conquer them, as mesmerism has done. Certain spirit-conditions are coming to be rationalized. In this country, for instance, the spirits of Indians everywhere manifest themselves, especially in connection with the cures of disease. The reason is simple. Indians were close to the earth, near to nature, in their lives, and they enjoy the scene of their old 'hunting grounds' more than such etherealized spirits as were slightly attached to it. But spirit-aid in therapeutics is mostly co-operative. Essential physicians, whether in our state of being or the higher state, feel an interest in their pursuit, and practise it. The most intelligent guide their assistants; but robust spirits of earthly qualities and attractions sometimes furnish a basic healing force that is almost physical."

Prof. P.'s system of healing is remarkable enough in all ways; but his claims for his "sensitized devices" would be too astounding for credence were it not that the things appear "to work," just as he says they will. Seemingly, they are nothing but small metallic plates; but they are charged, he affirms, with earth-magnetism as a "power-house," and then with animal magnetism, with natural human healing quality, with attractiveness to spirit-co-operation in that quality, and finally with psychic power and control—that is, direction of mind and will. In other words, Prof. P. says that, after twenty years of study and experiment he can transmit to his "sensitized devices," and store in them, all the four great healing agencies which can be employed in therapeutics apart from ordinary medicines.

By such means, he affirms, "not only healing, but instantaneous healing," to the extent at least of immediate relief from pain, can always be effected in all cases adapted to his treatment.

"Christian Science," he says—"mind-cure—faith-cure—oh yes, they 'demonstrate' over things, as the phrase goes. I admit it, at least in some instances. But, at their very best, they all *take time*. The patient must wait to exalt himself into some vision or condition he is told about, or to accept some theological doctrine or other, whether true or false. Suppose a man is knotted up with rheumatism, has a fit, or is insane. I don't wait for him to build up a belief, or to get into harmony with the Highest. I take him just as he is, clap my sensitizers on him, go to work myself, and, if he is not too far gone for aid on earth, I restore an equilibrium of body and brain. If I do this—if I instantly drive away the worst kind of pain—if I retrieve lost consciousness or a disordered mind—I can put faith enough into my patient for a beginning. Later, I will attend to his theology to the extent of my knowledge, if he desires my services as a priest."

The operation of Prof. P.'s sensitized appliances, according to his claim for them, is correction and vitalization of both mind and body, when disarranged or "ill," and then concentration of power in accordance with location of disease or pain. "As strange as it may seem," he says, "these little pieces of metal take upon themselves the physical and mental conditions of sickness, which can even be conveyed by them from one person to another, as I have proved by various experiments. But these conditions can be discharged from the plates, or 'grounded,' like electricity, and this, too, without destroying the higher, firmer, normal charge of health and strength.

"Do you look incredulous; do you smile with a tinge of pity?" asked Prof. P., as he talked. "Wait a minute. You have heard of Dr. Luys, one of the most distinguished physicians in the world, Charcot's favorite assistant, and now the head of the great Charity Hospital of Paris. Not long ago he had a patient—a young woman who had suffered nervous prostration, and was losing her mind from melancholia. She was affectionate, and greatly attached to her family. But she became aware that her love was strangely turning to aversion, which she could not control. Frightened and ashamed, she went to Dr. Luys. He tried everything he could think of to cure her, but unavailingly. At his wits' end—not knowing *what* to do—he took up, one day, a large electro-magnet, and, as a pure experiment of impulse, fastened it to her head. He was suddenly called away for three-quarters of an hour. Returning, he found his patient weak, but her head better and clearer than usual. Dismissing her, he put the magnet on his own head, took the chair she had sat in, and remained there as long as she had done. He then went to dine with his wife and children, of whom he is very fond. But, greatly to his surprise, he found that, with no fault of their own, they were not agreeable to him. *He had taken the conditions of his patient.*

"He was keen enough to recognize the fact, and announce it to his profession and the world. He drew the conclusion that the electro-magnet can absorb morbid brain-influences. Also that it can transfer such influences from the sick to the well, though two healthy persons are not affected by it. He added that the transference of conditions from the healthy to the diseased almost always benefits them.

"I am not hanging on 'high authorities,'" continued the Professor, "but they are sometimes useful to me. There is Dr. Julius Althaus, of Berlin, a member, too, of the English Royal College of Physicians. As explained in a recent issue of the *Lancet*, the chief English organ of the medical fraternity, Dr. Althaus is now rejuvenating old age, and prolonging our present term of life, by certain galvano-electric appliances—which, by the way, he does not tell quite all about. Henry Irving is understood to have been held back from the infirmities of advancing years, and restored to the stage, by Dr. Althaus."

Prof. P. claims to have been at work half a life-time in the general direction indicated by the experiments and achievements of Luys and Althaus, but to have been so busy that he has had no time to think about a degree of M. D. "The world," he says, "should be very grateful to these eminent gentlemen, and *I* certainly am grateful; for though I anticipated the happenings of Dr. Luys by several years, and though almost any 'magnetic healer' would assert the *hypothesis*, at least, of Dr. Althaus, my own theories and results are so far beyond my epoch that without the steps, however short, taken by such men as Luys and Althaus, I could get no sort of hearing. I am often laughed at, of course, as a 'crank'; but I generally laugh last—for, as the phrase goes nowadays, I 'get there.'"

CHAPTER XX.
CONCLUSION.

The moral of our story is an old one, always new. "There are more things in heaven and earth than" — anybody short of Mary Baker G. Eddy can put into a "science." From this text it would be logical to educe a cyclopedia every month or so. But one little point will do here.

The practise of medicine, notwithstanding its grand achievements, is still in its infancy. When I am ill, I call a doctor — the best in the vicinity. It is the custom; and, as Montaigne said, *Que sais-je?* I am not sure of much, and when I have "*grippe*" I am quite certain of less than ever. But the materials I have lately been at work on make me wish that "my doctor," instead of scorning all new things, would look into some of them, and add them to his acquirements. He will have no need to accept "Christian Science," which has been accurately described as "a way of getting cured of things by believing something that isn't true." I must excuse "my doctor" from accepted that inverted "science." But the general subject of occult and psychic healing is worthy of his attention. "My doctor" knows much: but, if he should enlarge his knowledge just a little, my faith in him would stand the increment.

One thing I shall insist on. "My doctor" must not endeavor to supersede Torquemada, Henry the Eighth, and the learned ecclesiastical doctors of the Inquisition. He must not interfere with the right of private judgment in saving the body, as they did in saving the soul. In such a case I should count them his superiors, inasmuch as the soul is really worth more than its external machinery, which, in a few years, more or less, must wear out and go to the cemetery.

The Inquisition honestly held a theory that the soul could only be saved by accepting a certain creed, and ought to be saved even at the cost of breaking the body on a wheel. The Inquisition would have been right, if its creed had really been the thing supposed. But four centuries of Protestantism have established a different theory: it is that, whatever any creed may be or do, every man has the prerogative of deciding for himself the manner of thinking which shall raise him to heaven or lower him to sheol. Still, I repeat, the soul is worth more than the body, and if Protestantism applies to the greater, it should apply to the less.

Some things have been settled, I suppose, by long experience, and have become matters of law for the protection of nations. Civilization requires that a man who knows nothing of physiology shall not practise surgery; that scarlet fever shall be quarantined; that school-children shall be saved from small-pox by vaccination. Medical degrees certify that the holders have studied medicine long enough at least to know something about it in a way that the common judgment recognises. Nothing is to be said against such requirements impartially applied to a whole people. They simply must be enforced. Christian Science opposes them, dodges them when it can; for it holds that human beings have no bodies except reflections of a wretched lie called "mortal mind." In spite of its source, this dangerous form of insanity should be dealt with as gently as possible, but certainly should not go unrestrained.[59] Let it conform to laws, not special to any religion or to any humbug masquerading as a religion, but general to the citizens who compose a free and sane community.

THE END

---

[59] These words were written long before Dr. Alan McLane Hamilton testified, in the Surrogate's Court, (New York City, Feb. 18th, 1901), that sincere Christian Scientists are afflicted with a form of insane delusion.

Lector House believes that a society develops through a two-fold approach of continuous learning and adaptation, which is derived from the study of classic literary works spread across the historic timeline of literature records. Therefore, we aim at reviving, repairing and redeveloping all those inaccessible or damaged but historically as well as culturally important literature across subjects so that the future generations may have an opportunity to study and learn from past works to embark upon a journey of creating a better future.

This book is a result of an effort made by Lector House towards making a contribution to the preservation and repair of original ancient works which might hold historical significance to the approach of continuous learning across subjects.

HAPPY READING & LEARNING!

LECTOR HOUSE LLP
E-MAIL: lectorpublishing@gmail.com